WOODLAND WALKS OF PEMBROKESHIRE

Woodland Walks of Pembrokeshire

David and Faith Bowers

© Text: David and Faith Bowers

All rights reserved.
No part of this publication may be reproduced,
stored in a retrieval system, or transmitted in any form, or by any means,
electronic, electrostatic, magnetic tape, mechanical, photocopying,
recording, or otherwise, without prior
permission of the author of the works herein.

ISBN: 978-1-84524-582-5

Published with the financial support of the Books Council of Wales.

Cover design: Lynwen Jones
The front cover shows part of the path alongside
the River Gwaun. The back picture is of Canaston Wood
on a misty day, with an inset of acorns.

Published by Gwasg Carreg Gwalch 2021
12 Iard yr Orsaf, Llanrwst, Wales LL26 0EH
☎ 01492 642031
books@carreg-gwalch.cymru
website: www.carreg-gwalch.cymru

Published and printed in Wales

*For all our friends in Pembrokeshire
and all who enjoy a good woodland walk*

Contents

Introduction		8
The Walks		11
WALK 1	**Aber Mawr**	14
	Identifying trees	18
WALK 2	**Llanychaer**	19
	Birch	22
	River meanders	23
WALK 3	**Nevern**	25
	Sycamore	30
	Still Learning	31
WALK 4	**Pengelli Forest**	32
	Hawthorn	37
	Measuring the height of Trees	38
WALK 5	**Cilgerran**	39
	Beech	46
WALK 6	**Pontfaen**	47
	Holly	52
	Gwaun Valley New Year	53
WALK 7	**Tŷ Canol woods**	54
	Clock of Ages	59
	Oak	60
WALK 8	**Brandy Brook**	61
	Elder	65
	The age of trees	66

WALK 9	Treffgarne Gorge	67
	Hazel	73
WALK 10	Pickle Wood	74
	Horse Chestnut	79
	Oxygen Factories	79
WALK 11	Canaston Woods	81
	Rowan	87
WALK 12	Minwear Forest	88
	The Swaying of Trees	92
	Alder	93
WALK 13	Little Milford	94
	Ash	99
	How does water get to the top of a tree?	100
WALK 14	Lawrenny Wood	102
	Lime	107
WALK 15	Amroth	108
	The structure of trees	112
WALK 16	Stackpole (northern section)	114..
	Sweet Chestnut	121
	The Da Vinci Code	122
WALK 17	Stackpole (southern section)	124
	Green spaces	131
Bibliography		133

Introduction

Pembrokeshire, in the south-west corner of Wales, has a beautiful, rugged coastline and fine sandy beaches. Visitors come from all over the world to walk the undulations of the coast path and enjoy the views. There is more to Pembrokeshire than its coast, though. There are excellent walks inland, along woodland trails following tumbling streams and through ancient forests. The aim of this book is to tell you about some of these. A good walk is made better, we are convinced, if it has a section through a wood. Trees provide walkers with shelter and interest. In bad weather, they protect us from wind and rain and on a hot summer's day they give welcome shade. Walking through a wood lets you hear and see birds and other animals at close hand.

The trees themselves are a sight to be enjoyed. Their greenery is soothing to the eye and, when accompanied by a decking of spring flowers, the whole picture is a delight. There are about one hundred common tree species in the UK and if, like us, you are not an expert, it can be fun to try to identify some of them. It is also interesting to see their appearance change with the seasons. We have included some basic notes about identifying a few of the more common types in the book.

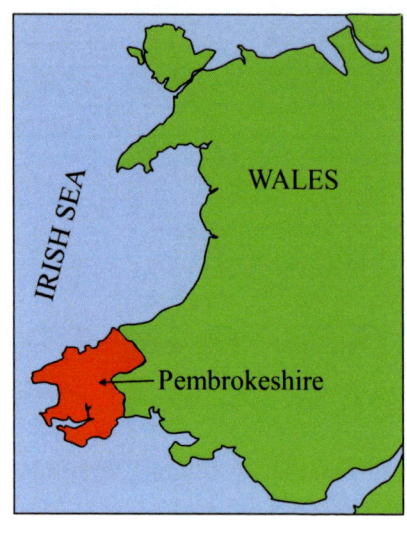

Trees are the oldest and largest living things on earth. Oak trees in an ancient Celtic rainforest can be several hundred years old; they have lived through many important events in the country's history. A mature oak may be 40 metres tall and spread almost as wide. It will weigh several tonnes. For some people, being close to such magnificent creatures inspires their curiosity. Where does the material that makes the tree come from? How do water and nutrients from the ground get to the top of the tree? Do trees live in splendid isolation, or are they aware of other trees around them? Is there a pattern to the structure of trees? Some of these questions have not yet been answered, but the questions, we think, are all interesting. You will find notes on these - and other questions that piqued our curiosity - in this book.

Most people in Wales are just a short distance away from a good woodland walk. Trees flourish in this country so long as they are given a chance to establish themselves and are left alone. In the 20th century, new forests of mostly non-native conifers, were planted all over our countryside. In the 21st century, many of these conifers are slowly being replaced with native species. Organisations such as the Woodland Trust Coed Cadw are preserving native forests and planting new ones. Our woodlands are under constant threat, though. More profit is available in using the land for housing and agriculture than in letting trees grow. By using our forests for recreation, we are giving local authorities and politicians good reason to conserve them.

There are some essentials to take on any forest walk. Dress for the weather and wear stout boots. The paths can be muddy and slippery, so take care. A walking stick or two makes for extra support. Woodlands have their own particular hazard: it is easy to become disorientated, we found. Paths can look confusingly similar and it is hard to keep a sense of direction when you are surrounded by trees. When you realise you are lost, it is hard not to panic and strike out in any direction, rather than stay put and think. The solution is easy: take a map and compass. We were never without one of the two Ordnance Survey Explorer maps of Pembrokeshire and we took a small GPS tracker. We always knew where we were on the map and, with the compass, could figure out which way we needed to go.

Pembrokeshire has a rich and fascinating history. Today, it is a green and pleasant rural county but, in the past, it was surprisingly industrial. On the walks you will come across abandoned coal mines and ruined water mills. Isambard Kingdom Brunel began, but didn't finish, a railway line through the county and you can see remnants of that, as well as evidence of the trans-Atlantic electric telegraph cable along which Queen Victoria sent a message to the President of the United States. There are ancient churches, some with stones from the earliest Christian times marked in Ogham script. There are tracks and resting places for pilgrims on their way to St David's cathedral. The county hosted an important centre for the support of knights on their way to, or returning from, the Crusades and there is evidence of that on these walks. You will also see the remains of several iron-age forts and a burial chamber older than the pyramids.

Some place names in Pembrokeshire have several versions. The destination of the first walk, for instance, appears as Aber Mawr in some sources and as Abermawr in others. We have used the version that appears on the OS maps (Aber Mawr in this case). We have tried to make the walk circular if possible, so that you don't have to cover the same ground twice. Directions are given for each walk, including details of public transport where available, parking places and, in some cases, we tell you where you might find refreshments afterwards. Two maps are included; one, based on the OS map, shows the walk in the context of its surroundings, with directions and distances represented correctly. The other, more like the London Underground map, illustrates each walk as an idealised strip or loop with features such as gates and fingerposts marked to help you fix your location. Note, though, that things change. On our visits, we would occasionally come across officials changing the signing on the path. Some signposts disappeared and new ones sprung up in different places.

A walk in the woods is a delight for all the senses. The air is fresh and the environment quiet and peaceful. Woodland paths are generally well-marked and maintained. A guide book is useful, but the best thing is to get out there amongst the trees and fresh air and enjoy yourself.

The Walks

Walk number	Name	Distance (km)	Time (hours)	Short Description
1	Aber Mawr	3	1	A gentle walk to a lovely beach.
2	Llanychaer	5	1.5	A stroll up and down part of the beautiful Gwaun valley.
3	Nevern	4	2	A circular walk along country lanes, bridleways and woodland paths with some steep sections.
4	Pengelli Forest	5	2	Mostly on single-file forest paths with some farm tracks.
5	Cilgerran	7	3	Mostly a circular walk on country lanes, bridleways and woodland paths.
6	Pontfaen	6.5	2.5	A walk up and down a beautiful river valley, on woodland paths and a country lane. Some steep climbs.
7	Tŷ Canol woods	6.5	2.5	A journey through one of the finest stretches of ancient oak woodland in the country.
8	Brandy Brook	4.5	1.5	A charming walk along the banks of a stream and past an old corn mill.
9	Treffgarne Gorge	7.5	3	A circular walk along both sides of the western Cleddau alongside the railway line leading to Fishguard.
10	Pickle Wood	8	3	A good walk to stretch your legs and burn off some calories
11	Canaston Woods	5	2	A circular route taking in the remains of a 12th century chapel and an Iron Age fort.
12	Minwear Forest	7	2.5	Mostly level, with occasional dips into a valley to cross a stream by a wooden bridge or boardwalk.
13	Little Milford	3	1.5	A short walk with some steep sections and plenty of historical interest.
14	Lawrenny Wood	5	2	A charming circular walk which packs a surprising amount of variety into its short length.
15	Amroth	7	2.5	Inland from the beach alongside tumbling streams and wooded marshland.
16	Stackpole (north)	7.5	2.5	A circuit on woodland paths.
17	Stackpole (south)	5.5	2	A walk along lake shores, mostly in woodland, with a visit to a cracking beach.

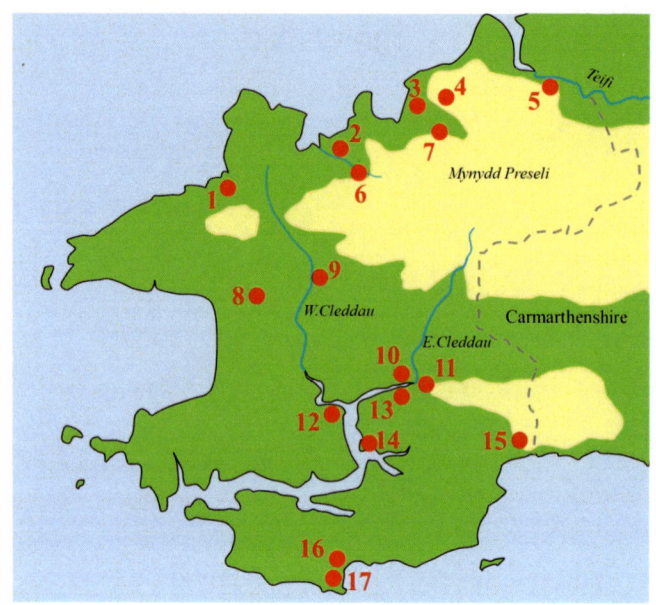

The walks. Cream coloured areas represent land over 400 feet.

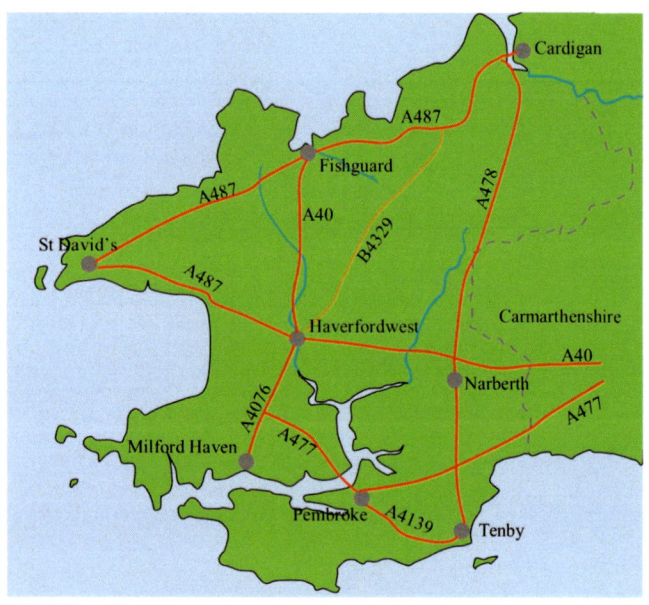

Major roads and towns of Pembrokeshire

The Walks

WALK 1	Aber Mawr		WALK 10	Pickle Wood
WALK 2	Llanychaer		WALK 11	Canaston Woods
WALK 3	Nevern		WALK 12	Minwear Forest
WALK 4	Pengelli Forest		WALK 13	Little Milford
WALK 5	Cilgerran		WALK 14	Lawrenny Wood
WALK 6	Pontfaen		WALK 15	Amroth
WALK 7	Tŷ Canol woods		WALK 16	Stackpole (north)
WALK 8	Brandy Brook		WALK 17	Stackpole (south)
WALK 9	Treffgarne Gorge			

Symbols used on maps

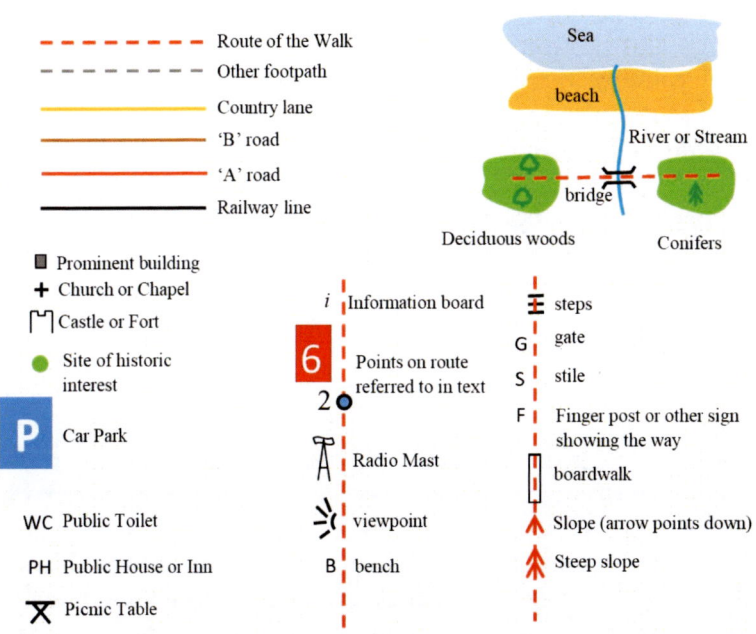

Walk 1 Aber Mawr

This is a gentle, circular, wooded walk to a lovely beach. Distance 3 km; allow an hour or a little more.

Aber Mawr is one of the finest beaches on the north Pembrokeshire coast. It is not easy to get to by road and so it is also one of the quietest. This stroll through the woods and back will get you there in a very pleasant way  and, on a hot day, you can cool off with a swim in the sea.

The T11 bus running between St David's and Fishguard will drop you at Mathry village. From the main road (A487) where the lane leads up to the Farmer's Arms, look for the sign to Preseli Venture and follow this narrow road to the start of the walk. If you are driving, take the turning for Mathry from the A487 and immediately turn right onto the road to Preseli Venture. Pass this outdoor activity centre and the farm and take the next turning on the left. Immediately on the right, in the hollow, you will find a parking space in the shade of the trees and big enough for one car at **1** (SM 8881 3350).

Starting from the small parking space, return the few yards to the road junction, turn left and walk up the lane. Pass a signposted path on your left and carry on to the top of the hill where you come across a path crossing the lane with a fingerpost pointing in both directions (**2** 8873 3369). Turn left on to the path here and you are immediately plunged into woodland, with the path leading steadily downhill. The trees are a mixture of sycamore, ash, holly, oak and hawthorn. Watch out for the tree roots which lie across the path and are a trip hazard.

Continue on this path for about one kilometre, walking along the top of the slope leading down into the valley to your left. You will pass a junction at **3** (8865 3895) where there is a path leading into a field to your right and down into the woods to the left. Soon after this, there is a dip and S-bend on the path, which can get slippery when wet. We came across a stone wall, with an old gate on the right, mostly covered in greenery. The first view of the sea is magical, sparkling blue water low down between the tree tops. Pass through a kissing gate and there are two ways to go from here. One is to take the path leading down to your left and across an open field to the beach. The other is to follow the path to the right which will take you across some open fields past a substantial ruin and down to the sea. The top of the beach is pebbly but a sandy, lower section, is exposed when the tide is out. On very low tides, a sunken forest can be seen at the very edge of the beach.

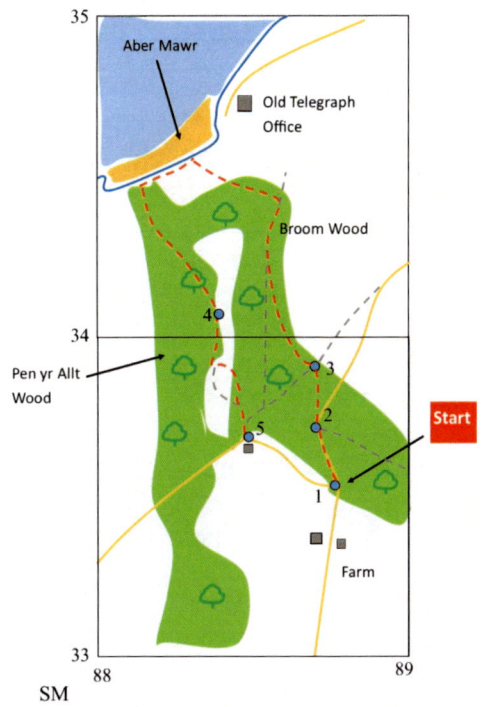

Aber Mawr beach has a place in the history of telecommunications. In the 1860's an electrical cable ran ashore here and continued up the slope to the east to a telegraph office (the building is still there and is now run as a holiday home). A cable went from this office to London and another cable crossed the Irish Sea to a point between Rosslare and Wexford, following the route now travelled by the Stena ferry. The telegraph cable crossed Ireland as far as Valencia where it joined the cable running along the floor of the Atlantic Ocean to Trinity Bay in Newfoundland. This quiet spot at Aber Mawr was an important link in the chain that allowed telegraph messages to pass between New York and London. One hundred years after the United States of America declared its independence from the British Crown, Queen Victoria sent a message of goodwill to the American President in  the form of electrical signals passing along a wire under this beach.

The messages were sent as pulses of electricity, short and long, in Morse code. The technology was very challenging, first in laying the cable and afterwards in using it. The matter drew the attention of the best engineers and scientists of the day. Throughout its life,  the telegraph cable was the servant of governments and business. Ordinary people continued to communicate across the Atlantic in the old way: in hand-written letters sent by ship. The electric telegraph service at Aber Mawr continued in use until a storm in the winter of 1922 destroyed the cable.

Continue the walk westward (with the sea on your right) along the top of the shingle bank until its end where you will see one path (the coast path) leading straight ahead. There are two paths leading inland, to your left. The first is marked by a finger post but gets very muddy in winter. It is better to take the second unmarked path just a few yards further on. This follows a higher route and keeps out of the bog. Keep to the upper path for as long as you can, passing an old quarry on your right and what looks like two venerable (and well-constructed) gate posts. The woods here have the feel of an ancient oak

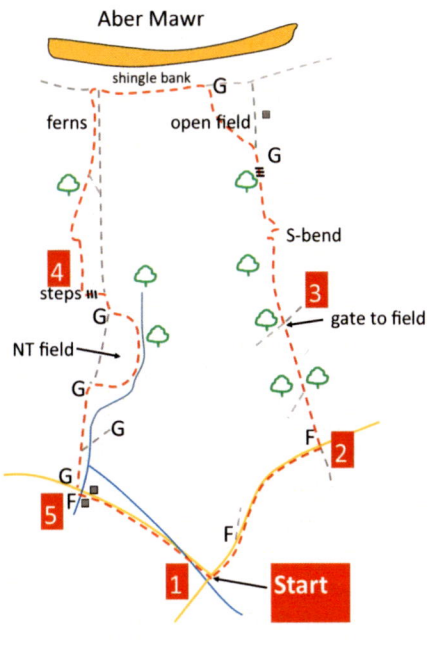

forest, which is probably what they are. We came across a sweet chestnut tree with its long, serrated leaves still orange in mid-November. In a short while you will come to some steps leading down to the left (at **4** SM 8842 3408). Walk down these to join the lower path. There is a gate here into a field (owned by the National Trust). You can choose to walk across the field or follow the path that goes around the edge of the field. Either way brings you to a straight track leading, through a gate at **5** (8847 3373), to a lane. Turn left here, pass some cottages and walk along the lane, with a stream on your left, back to the start of the walk.

After finishing the walk, you can treat yourself to refreshments at Tregwynt Woolen Mill (SM 8940 3485). This is a working mill in which you can watch machines weaving blankets and other products. The mill has a café selling snacks and hot meals and there is plenty of room to sit inside and out. There is a shop and you can have a look around the mill. Today the looms are run by electricity, but the old water turbine, which used to provide the power, is on display.

Identifying trees

We were certainly not experts at identifying trees when we finished this book but we were better than when we started. Knowing what kind of tree you are looking at and anticipating how it will change over the year adds enjoyment to a woodland walk. When you have been bitten by the naming bug, you may find that you are drawn to look at trees in other places, in a supermarket car park or someone else's garden, to test your new-found knowledge.

The feature that most people will start with is the leaves, but there are other important clues to a tree's identity. The fruits and nuts that develop in autumn are a great help as are the flowers in spring. In some trees, the bark is a giveaway, for example in a silver birch. Once you have made a clear identification, you can make visit your tree at different times of year to see how it changes.

One problem we found is that in their natural environment in a woodland, different kinds of tree grow close together, sometimes with their branches overlapping. It can be difficult to match the trunk with the leaves that dangle in front of your face. The problem is exacerbated by ivy and other climbers on the trunk and branches. Making a trip to a botanical garden is a good way to see healthy specimens in isolation. We also found it helpful to join the Woodland Trust and take with us their handy identification guide on these walks.

| Walk 2 | Llanychaer |

A lovely stroll up and down part of the beautiful Gwaun valley. Distance for the return journey is about 5 km. The walk is mostly level; allow an hour and a half.

This is a charming walk. It takes you for one and a half miles along the northern bank of the river Gwaun (pronounced to rhyme with 'wine'). The path stays close to the water for most of the way and under a canopy of trees for most of the time.

You will be accompanied by song birds, the tumbling sound of the river as it makes its way to the sea at Fishguard, the crunch of your boots on the footpath and the occasional greeting of other walkers. Everyone we met was enjoying this walk. On a sunny spring day when the light filters down through tall trees onto flowing water and beds of wild garlic, it is truly delightful.

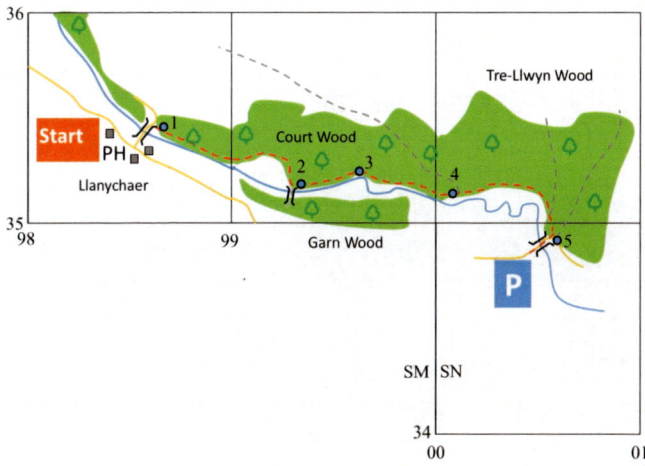

The walk begins at the small hamlet of Llanychaer. There is limited parking outside the pub, the Bridge End Inn, and there are handy picnic tables nearby where you can sit to put your boots on. Take the lane opposite the pub and cross the river by the old stone bridge, then take the footpath on your right, through the gate at **1** (SM 9873 3548). You are quickly into a fine woodland walk with a level path and a good mixture of trees: sycamore, holly, beech and more. After a while, the path leaves the river and you have a climb up to the left. At the top, your way leads to the right and gently descends back down to river level. There are steep slopes up to your left all along here and taking paths that lead in that direction is only recommended if you are feeling energetic.

In a little while you come to a clearing at **2** (SM 9943 3519), where there is a bench where you can have a picnic, or just sit and admire the trees. If you are lucky, you might see a kingfisher here; they like this spot too. There is a wooden bridge crossing the river - the path across the bridge will take you back to the main road to Llanychaer if you have had enough at this point. It is a bit of a

scramble, though, to get back to the road. If you carry on along the river you will soon come to some rapids which are picturesque enough for a calendar photo (at **3**, SM 9966 3524).

Shortly afterwards the path emerges through a gate with an open field on your right, between you and the river, and woodland to your left. Fencing separates you from the field and the path climbs gently to the corner at **4** (SN 0014 3520), where there is a path leading off to the left. Keep straight on along the river and as the path climbs a little here you get to see some good examples of river meanders. Most rivers form bends or meanders if they are flowing across a flat piece of ground and they have room enough either side. If you walk down to the river here you can see some nice details repeated on each of the bends. The river bank on the outer curve of the bend forms a steep cliff, where the soil is being eroded and carried away by the stream. On the inner side of the bend, there is a small beach of pebbles which have been left here as the water leaves the bend. Over time, the erosion of the outer bank and the addition of solid material to the inner bank will make the meander grow.

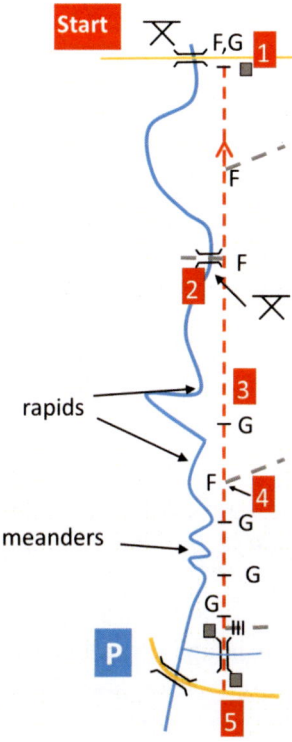

Soon after the meanders you pass through two gates and come across another path for the energetic, leading off to the left and up the hill, beginning with some steps this time. You are now approaching the end of this particular walk. You pass by some cottages, cross a fast-flowing stream and reach the road at 5 (SN 0064 3492). The lane crosses the river at Cilrhedyn Bridge and close by there is a car park, a telephone kiosk (no longer operational) and a post box. There is quite a bit of social history in these two red boxes. The changeable slotted signs on the post box (that tell the times of the next collection) are in Welsh and English. The original signs – the Royal Crest, the words LETTERS ONLY and NEXT COLLECTION, which are cast into the iron box are in English only. The official view of the importance of the Welsh language has changed since King George VI was on the throne. Across the lane is a classic red telephone box with a practical and elegant dome-shaped roof. This also bears a crown, from the time when telephones were run by the General Post Office and were a national asset. This box probably goes back to the time when the cost of a call was four old pennies and you pressed button A when your call was answered or button B to get your money back if it was not. Now there is no telephone in the box at all. The box is empty and rather sad-looking. It was probably never very well used – there are just a few scattered houses in the area – but it is possible to imagine a farmer turning out here on a cold and wet night to make an emergency call for the midwife.

After the walk, the Bridge End Inn is well worth a visit. It is popular with locals and, in summer, with the campers in the field opposite. The landlord, Paul, will make you welcome. Good conversation is available and refreshing, tasty beer from the Gwaun Valley brewery.

Birch

Birch trees grow everywhere. They are quick to colonise new land. When Britain was connected to the continent of Europe, birch forests (hiding wooly mammoths) grew on the land bridge. We know that because fragments of fossilised birch are occasionally brought up by trawlers from the bed of the North Sea. Look out for pointed leaves, with *serrated* edges (like a saw). Sometimes you will notice 4 or 5 big teeth along the edge of the leaf with smaller

teeth growing on them. Silver birches have a smooth leaf stalk and downy birches have hairs on the stalk. Both types of birch develop catkins in the spring. Male (long) and female (short) catkins grow on the same tree. Birches have a shiny light grey or silvery trunk. As the tree matures, the trunk develops dark horizontal stripes. These are lenticels, or fissures in the bark, and are used for gas exchange.

River meanders

Like old acquaintances forming their conversation over a cup of tea, rivers tend to meander. All rivers, large and small, have this tendency and the meanders have the same shape, however big the river. To be exact, the wavelength of the meanders – the distance from one curved bit to the next – increases in proportion to the width of the river. The meanders on a small stream would look much like those on a large river if both were drawn on scales so that they could be overlapped. Nature has clearly found a pattern here that works.

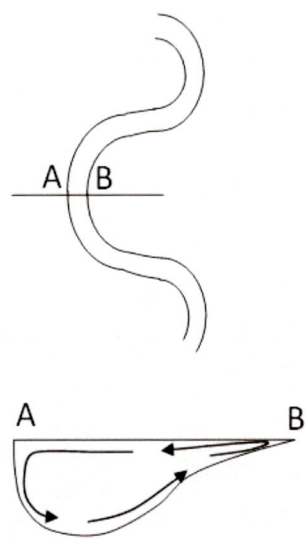

The formation of river meanders is believed to go something like this. When water flows around a river bend, the forces acting on the water produce something called a *secondary circulation*: a flow at right angles to the main direction of the current (see picture). In the secondary circulation, surface water moves towards the outside of the bend where it sinks and then flows back to the opposite bank as a bottom flow. This circulation is superimposed on the main downstream current, so a parcel of water follows a helical, or corkscrew, path. As it dives down the outer bank of the bend, the current erodes soil and stones making a steep cliff. The eroded material is then caried down and across the stream where it is deposited on the inner bank of the next bend. In this way an initially small and localised deviation in the river can grow into a meander which creates other meanders further downstream. The growth continues until the meanders are so large that the tendency for the stream to cut across in a straight line from one loop to the next can no longer be resisted. Then the whole process starts again.

The curvy parts of the meanders have a shape similar to part of the circumference of a circle, but there are also straight parts of the river where the bends change direction. Mathematicians have been attracted to the problem of finding a formula for this shape and an explanation of why it is so similar on rivers of all sizes. One suggestion is that the river finds the shape which takes the least energy to make the water flow around the curves and in which the energy loss is distributed uniformly along the stream, but no-one really knows.

| Walk 3 | **Nevern** |

A circular walk along country lanes, bridleways and woodland paths with some steep sections. Distance 4 km; allow 2 hours.

This walk starts in the village of Nevern in north Pembrokeshire and takes you on what is believed to be an ancient pilgrimage route along the banks of the river Nyfer. Nevern is surely one of the prettiest villages in Pembrokeshire, tucked away out of sight of

the traffic travelling on the main Cardigan to Fishguard road. The village has a fine Norman church, a community hall, some quaint cottages and a pub. This is a great place to start and finish a walk. The going is mainly easy, under trees and along a river bank but it can get wet in places, especially in winter, and there are some scrambles up and down a slope. The T5 Traws Cymru bus, or the smaller local service called the Poppit Rocket, will drop you at Temple Bar on the A487 and it is less than 1 km from there to Nevern. Alternatively, you can drive to the village, taking the B4582

from Temple Bar. The church makes a good place to start: there is parking space for a car, and a mounting block which offers a seat while you put on your boots. A curious robin perched close to watch us doing this. The churchyard has a fine Celtic cross and an ancient stone with the rare Ogham script. Toilets are available behind the village hall, which is near to the church.

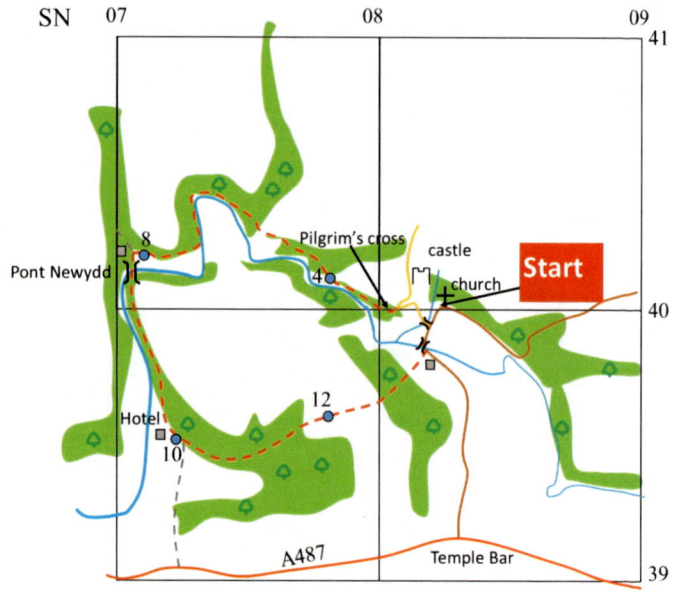

From the church at **1** (SN0832 3998) set out with the stream on your right and take the first lane on the right to cross the bridge. Follow this lane past some cottages and with views over an open field to the church. The lane then twists its way uphill. The footpath that we will take leaves the road at the first sharp right bend (**2** 0812 4001) but you may want to carry on the a little further up the hill to look at Nevern Castle (Castell Nanhyfer on the OS map) which lies beyond the next bend of the road. Nevern was a motte and bailey castle. A motte is a mound on which was built a wooden or stone keep. The bailey was a walled courtyard around the motte. Motte and bailey castles were introduced to Britain by the Normans; Windsor Castle in England is a famous example. The one at Nevern was built (on the site of an earlier Welsh fortification) in the 12th century by Robert Fitzmartin, who

was sent to impose Norman rule on this part of Wales. Not much remains of the castle – much of the original structure was built of wood – but the earth mounds that formed the motte are still impressive.

Return down the lane to **2** and walk up the ramp to join the signposted path. On your right here is Nevern's famous pilgrims cross. The cross, cut into the rock face, is of unknown date but is believed to be associated with the pilgrim's journey from the Abbey at Strata Florida in Ceredigion to St David's Cathedral in Pembrokeshire. Below the cross, there is a small level platform on the rock which looks as though it could have been used as a seat. Two workmen from the National Park authority were replacing a signpost by the cross when we arrived. They had worked out a way of getting the old stump out with the minimum of fuss and were pleased about that.

After a short walk through a woodland popular with songbirds, the path comes to a gate at 3 (SN 0799 4004) leading into an open field. Walk around the edge of this field for 200 metres or so to a

stile at **4** (SN 0776 4018) which takes you into a charming walk on a path above the rapids of the Nevern river. Climb up some steps to a stile at 5 (SN 0788 4024) which brings you to another open field which you cross, heading towards some buildings that you can see in a dip down to your left. We first did this walk in December during a hard frost and the ground here was hard as iron, the leaves lying on the ground trimmed in a hoar frost. A robin hopped towards us as we crossed the open ground.

Go through the gate at the far end of the field, straight across the lane in front of you and down a short stony path, turning right by the finger post, to the bridge over a small stream (**6** SN 0758 4034). Cross the bridge and go straight ahead on the narrow path down the side of a building on your left. The path now follows the banks of the river Nyfer. You pass a gate marked Private and then climb up the bank at the point where the river bends to the left. Some stone steps take you down to the river again and shortly you come to a ruined cottage at **7** (SN 0736 4029). The OS explorer map of North Pembrokeshire shows a path crossing the river from here and leading back to Nevern, but we could see no sign of this path and it would be difficult to cross the river at this point.

Continue on the path, past the outbuildings of the ruined cottage. A gap forms between you and the river bank for a while here; there is a field between you and the river to the left. Soon you come to the junction at **8** (SN 0717 4023) where you can turn left to cross the fine stone bridge (Bont Newydd) over the river. The road here is not tarmacked – just a bridleway really. The residents in the cottages nearby (and visitors to the caravans down to the right here) must need good suspension in their cars. Follow the bridleway straight ahead, with a wooded valley down to the right and an open field to the left to the junction at **9** (SN 0725 3960) where the path becomes concrete and then tarmacked. Pass the turning to the right, walking behind the hotel, unless you want to go in for a cup of tea. Llwyngwair Manor is now a hotel with expansive grounds used as a holiday park. There was a house here in medieval times but it was rebuilt in the early 18th century by the Bowen family. George Bowen (1722-1810) was a leading figure in the early Methodist church and John Wesley and other important Methodists came to stay here.

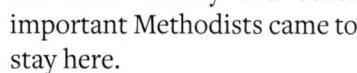

Follow the lane to **10** (SN 0724 3948) passing some large out-buildings on the left. Fork left here, taking the path leading into the woods. There is a gate which you can walk through or climb the steps at the side – an unusual arrangement. We noticed that quite a few deciduous trees in this wood still had their leaves in the week before Christmas. One oak tree towering above us had brown tips to its leaves but plenty of green too. Keep straight on at **11** (SN 0748 3943) and cross a  stream (frozen on the day of our visit). The path is wide here and covered with beech leaves. It has the feel of an estate bridleway, rather than a natural woodland path. Rhododendron bushes can be seen either side, so perhaps this was an old driveway between Nevern and Llwyngwair. The path ends at **12** (SN 0777 3956) where there are 3 gates. The left and right gates lead to fields. We took the centre gate and followed the path between high banks (an old Drover's track, perhaps?). The path re-enters the woods and dips down for a short distance to a gate at **13** (SN 0810 3968). We were struck, when opening these gates, at the fantastic patterns created by the frost on the tops of the gateposts.

Cross the field beyond the gate, heading for the buildings in front of you. Go through another gate at **14** (SN 0828 3980) to re-join the road. Turn left here to cross the bridge over the River Nyfer and pass the village hall on your way back to the church.

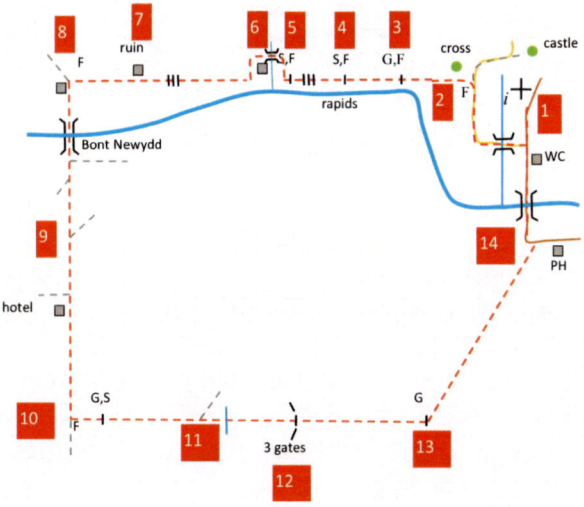

Sycamore

Sycamores have large five-pointed leaves, a little like the ones on the Canadian flag (maples and sycamores both belong to the Acer family). The trees are best known to young children for their helicopter seeds which fall in the Autumn. The spinning action of the helicopter wings slows the descent of the seeds, allowing them to be carried further by the wind. In this way, the seeds are spread well away from the parent plant; the young saplings won't be a competitor with the parent and the trees are able to colonise new areas. There is a clever bit of design in action here: the seed pods need a bit of shaking to dislodge them from their parent tree and so it is only on a breezy day (when the wind is there to carry them along) that they are launched into flight. The full pods are heavier than the wings, so the seed automatically orientates itself into spinning mode, heavy part down, wings up, no matter how it first starts to fall. It is likely that the real seeds have evolved to take full

advantage of the various tricks that aerodynamics offer so that they maximise the time that they are in the air. Nature has designed the perfect form for the job.

Sycamores are fast growing and tall; their wood makes an excellent fuel and it is sought after in furniture making. Not everyone appreciates a sycamore, though. They can be a nuisance in a garden, setting up fast growing seedlings in the lawn, but Robert Louis Stevenson included this tree in his evocative description of a wonderful home:

Go, little book, and wish to all
Flowers in the garden, meat in the hall
A bin of wine, a spice of wit,
A house with lawns enclosing it
A living river by the door
A nightingale in the sycamore!

Still Learning

Trees have been important to us ever since humans have walked on this planet yet, remarkably we are still learning new things about them. After the great storm that hit southern England in 1987, many damaged woodlands were restored by their owners, charities and public bodies, often at great expense. It soon became apparent, however, that woodlands that had been left alone were recovering just as well or even better than those that had been cleared and replanted. Nature can sometimes heal itself without our help.

Surely one of the most remarkable recent discoveries about trees is that they are not always out to compete for space and resources, but they can co-operate with each other. Suzanne Simard is a Canadian scientist who discovered that fungi and roots act as communication and transport routes between trees. Simard used carbon isotopes to measure the flow of material from one tree to another. She discovered that in a mixed woodland in winter, deciduous trees which are not able to photosynthesise receive a sugar supplement from evergreen trees. In summer, the roles are reversed and the broadleaved deciduous trees now provide a sugar supplement for evergreens.

Walk 4 Pengelli Forest

A circular walk of about 5 kilometres. Allow two hours. The walk is mostly on single-file forest paths with some farm tracks. There are one or two steepish climbs.

Pengelli forest is one of 76 National Nature Reserves in Wales, each of which is designated to conserve areas of wildlife, habitats and geological features of special interest. In the case of Pengelli, the NNR includes the largest ancient oak woodland in Pembrokeshire. It is managed by the Wildlife Trust of South and West Wales. The Trust produces a leaflet, available online, in which they lay out a series of circular walks which are also marked on clear maps distributed throughout the woods. Some walks are long, some short; each is given its own colour and marked by signs with the appropriate colour. We took the boundary walk which visits most parts of the woodland.

Getting to the start of this walk is part of the fun. The T5 bus running between Fishguard and Cardigan will drop you in Felindre Farchog. From here, head east on the A487 for a short while and take the lane heading off to the left at SN 105 390. It is about a mile and a half from here to the gate into the woods. If you are driving, it would be difficult to take this turning coming along the A487 from the other direction: it is too sharp. You have to approach the junction from the Felindre Farchog side. Head up the narrow lane through the trees, keeping an eye open for passing places in case you meet a car coming the opposite way. After a while you pass through a small farmyard with geese and ducks quacking on the road, splash through a ford and drive uphill. About 500 metres after the ford, the entrance to Pengelli Forest National Nature Reserve is on the right. There is parking here (SN 123 396) for about ten cars.

Enter the woods via the gate by the large sign for Pengelli Forest. Ignore the steps to your left and walk up the broad path in front of you. In 50 metres you come to a shelter with some benches, a map and information board. This is a good place to get oriented. Several paths converge here, but keep to the one straight ahead – the 'yellow' path in the colour convention of the Wildlife Trust map. The walk here is mainly through oak with ferns and shrubs beneath the tree canopy.

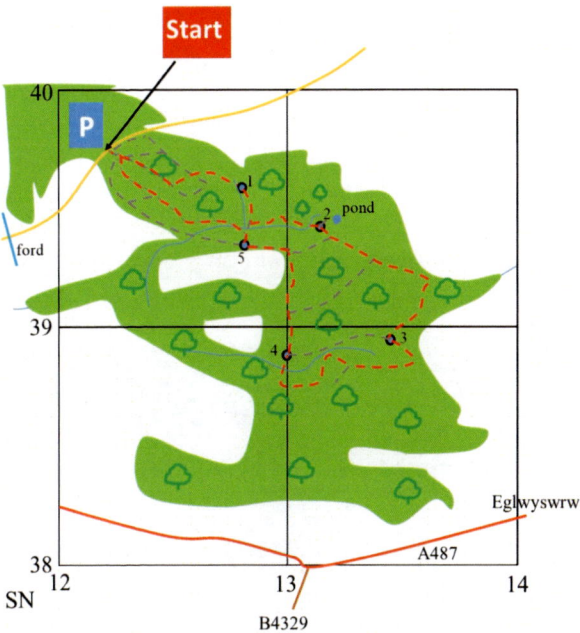

Pass a bench to the left and keep going to a fork where you bear left down the path coded brown (brown is reserved to mark short links between longer paths). After a short distance, turn right (onto the 'red' path). There is a gate to the side of the path here and a carved tree stump (one of several in these woods). Follow this path down into a dip and look out for the large fallen tree by a stream bed which can be dry in summer, at **1** (SN 1267 3957). The path

continues onwards here but soon runs into a dead end.

Turn right at the fallen tree to follow the path along a valley. Pass another bench on your left and cross a bridge to continue along a lovely walk with a stream on your right.

This part of the walk is marked as the 'Hawthorn field' in the leaflet produced by the Wildlife Trust. There are certainly lots of hawthorns here, including plenty of new growth. At the T junction turn left onto the 'green' path. There is another carving here, on your right. Follow the path uphill to another T junction where there were (at the time of our visit) some woodpiles. If you turn left here, you will soon arrive at the clearing where trees are being felled, but to continue the walk, turn right at this junction.

You soon come to another T-junction, where you turn left. Continue on to cross a small stream on the far side of which the path divides in two to pass either side of a large and imposing tree. At **2** (SN 1318 3943) turn right, keeping to the 'green' path. You are at the eastern edge of the wood here and you will catch glimpses of open fields to your left. In a while you come to a track that looks as though it is used by tractors. The signpost indicates the 'green' track is to the right and 'blue' to the left. Turn left, heading south. You pass a junction with a linking 'brown' path leading off to the right. This path has a name – the Midland Way -

on some of the maps, so-called because it is home to a variety of hawthorn called the Midland hawthorn. Taking this shortcut will take you home, but if you want the full experience continue on the blue path here, passing a carving on your left and crossing some board walks. The board walks continue intermittently on this path.

After a while, the path takes an s-bend over a wooden bridge crossing a stream. It feels like you are entering a wild part of the wood here. It is the remotest part of the walk and the least frequented, we suspect. It is fascinating but it is sometimes necessary to climb over (or under) trees that have fallen across the path. At **3** (SN 1345 3894), the path emerges from the trees to join a track. Turn left and follow the 'blue' track up the gradient to what is a little roundabout with trees forming the central island. Follow the track around to the right. A shelter is marked on the map at this point, but we didn't see it on our visit. The track takes you to a clearing; look out here for the fingerpost indicating where the 'blue' path leads off to the right into the woods. Take this path, crossing boardwalks and following the general gradient downhill. The path bends to the right and there is a short boardwalk bridge over a stream and then the path takes you up to a junction, once again, with a stony track (**4**, SN 1298 3897).

Turn left here and walk along the stony path, which twists and turns a little as it takes you uphill. On a summer's day, you can look

out for the wild flowers which decorate either side of this track. Some of these have a powerful scent which provides a welcome diversion on a hot day. The path brings you to a clearing with a woodshed containing stacks of drying timber. Turn left here and walk down the broad stony path to the shelter which makes a good spot for a picnic.

Follow the stony path downhill until, after a slight bend to the left, you come across a path to the right at **5**. Take this, walking downhill, and enjoy the feel of earth beneath your feet once more. It is a short linking path down some steps to a junction where you turn left and cross a stream. You are now back on the 'red' path which takes you along the side of a valley sloping down to your left. When you arrive at a fork, bear right to stay on the red path and take the steady climb past a clearing visible through the trees on your left. The path brings you back to the shelter near the start of the walk. Turn left here to get back to the road.

After the walk, the Iron Age village at Castell Henllys is worth seeing. The entrance by road is from the A487 between Felindre Farchog and Eglwyswrw. There is an entrance fee to the village itself but the small friendly café is free to enter and you can eat an ice cream or drink tea by the tumbling stream here. If you fancy something stronger, there is the Salutation Inn in Felindre Farchog.

Hawthorn

Hawthorns are commonly found in hedgerows; their sharp thorns form an excellent barrier against farm animals and humans. They are also ancient and native residents of our woodlands and there are plenty to be seen. The leaves are lobed, a little like small oak leaves, with a sawtooth pattern on the tip. The young leaves, formed in spring, are edible and pleasant to chew; you can try them out as you walk, or collect them for chopping in a salad. In May, the hawthorn tree is covered in beautiful white blossom – the May flower – and looks quite magnificent in full sun. The flowering of the May tree is traditionally taken as the change of spring to summer and the old saying 'don't cast a clout until May is out' probably refers to the opening of

the May blossom rather than the ending of the month. The fruits form as the blossom fades, green at first and ripening to red in the autumn. The red hawthorn berries, called haws, are an important source of winter food for birds, including migrating visitors such as Fieldfares and Redwings.

Measuring the height of Trees

The height of a tree can be measured by anyone at ground level using a technique which mathematicians call *similar triangles*. Similar triangles have the same shape but different sizes.

To find the height of a tree in the woods, you need to take a tape measure along in your bag. We identified a tall tree by a river and walked 32 paces away from the trunk. The exact distance you pace out will depend on what gets in the way and your ability to perform the next step accurately and comfortably. Point one arm to the top of the tree and the other to the roots (as in the picture) and get a friend to measure the distance x between your hands (which in this case was 23 inches) and the length of your arm (29 inches). If you are on your own, you can dangle a walking stick vertically from your top hand, note where the stick reaches your lower hand and measure that distance.

The large triangle which has the tree as its vertical side and you in the corner is a similar triangle to the one formed by your arms and the imaginary line, length x, between your hands. One triangle is a magnified version of the other and the sides are in the same ratio. If H is the height of the tree, then $H/32$ is equal to $23/29$. H is therefore 25 paces. Our paces are about a metre long, so the height of the tree we had chosen was 25 metres (about 82 feet).

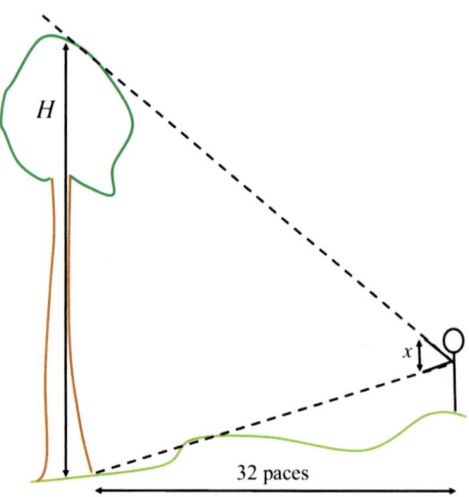

| Walk 5 | **Cilgerran** |

Mostly a circular walk on country lanes, bridleways and woodland paths. Distance about 7 km. Allow 3 hours, more if you plan to have lunch at the Wildlife Centre.

This walk takes you along the valley of the River Teifi, from Cilgerran to the Welsh Wildlife Centre. You pass a medieval castle and a stone marked with the ancient Ogham script. The path takes you through ancient woodland clinging to a steep-sided gorge above the river and there is the opportunity to see birds and river animals close up at the Wildlife Centre, where there is a shop and a cafe. It is possible to do this walk using only easy footpaths but the gorge walk, which is certainly very beautiful, is narrow and steep, and has a steep drop on one side. Good boots are needed if you choose the gorge walk and sticks gave us the confidence to tackle the slippy slopes.

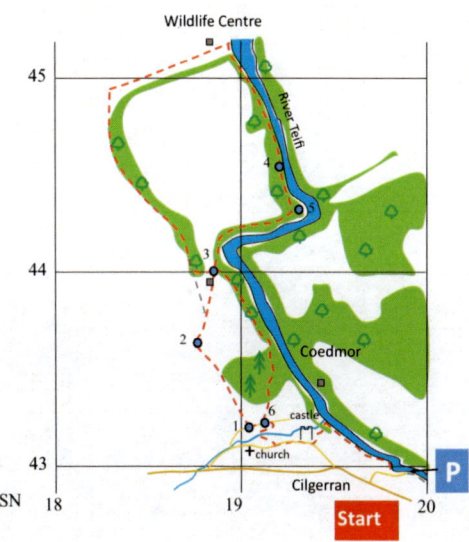

The walk begins at the village of Cilgerran. The 430 bus

service from Cardigan to Narberth will drop you in the village square. Alternatively, the car park (SN198 429) is reached by a narrow lane running down to the river from the main street (the village shop is on the corner). Here, there are public toilets, picnic tables and a display centre. This is a charming spot in its own right, made even more charming on the day of our visit by the robin that perched on the car's wing mirror as soon as we had parked. There are information boards on the building at the northern end of the car park telling of the Teifi valley's agricultural and industrial history and of the coracles that still use this river.

Set off north from the car park, with the river on your right. After a short distance, you reach a point where the path ahead is blocked by a tributary (the River Plysgog) joining the main river from the left. Our OS explorer map (OL35) shows a footpath here which continues along the river bank as far as Cardigan, but apparently this path has been closed for some time. There may be parts of it still functioning, but don't rely on it. The circular tower poking out above the trees on the far side of the river belongs to Coedmor Mansion. There is a story that, at one time long ago, a fishing net was stretched across the river here. A line attached to the net rang a bell in the mansion when salmon had been caught for tea.

On our side of the river there is the not so glamorous

water-works building. Take the steps that lead up from here to the walls of Cilgerran Castle, an ancient fortification which still plays a role in the community. At the time we visited in November, the gates were covered in Remembrance Day tributes. The lane that passes the castle gates ends in a T junction, where you turn right into Church Street. After 150 yards or so, you will see a signposted path descending steeply to your right. That is our route onwards, but if you have time, it is worth carrying on a little further along Church Street to the church itself, St. Llawddog's. The church is a handsome building and the churchyard is famous for its Ogham stone – one of several in Pembrokeshire.  The stone is thought to date from the 5th or 6th century, soon after the Romans left Britain. There is lettering on the stone in Latin, which translates as 'Tregussus, son of Macutreni, lies here', but there is also, on the side, some lettering in the ancient Ogham script which was brought to Wales from Ireland. Near this stone there is the grave of the man after whom the highest mountain in Canada is named. Who would have thought it, in a tiny churchyard in far-away Pembrokeshire? Mount Logan, in the far north-west of Canada, is nearly six times higher than Snowdon. The man himself, Sir William Logan, was born in Montreal in 1798 and became the founding director of the Geological Survey of Canada. When he retired, he came to spend the last few years of his life with his sister, Elizabeth Gower, who lived in Pembrokeshire. Sir William died in 1875 and was buried in St Llawddog's.

From the church, walk back down the lane the way you have come and this time take the signposted path down into the valley. The path is steep to begin with but there is a handrail. Walk to the bottom, cross the stream by the bridge and then climb the hill on the other side of the river, passing some pretty cottages. The path brings you out onto a lane. Turn left here, pass the first footpath leading off to the right, and continue until you come, at **1** (SN1905 4317) to a signposted bridleway on your right. Turn onto the bridleway, pass some unattractive farm structures and soon you come to a gate with a notice saying that this is the southern entrance to Fforest Farm. Keep on the broad track to a junction at **2** (1875 4368) where you turn right. Here we met a friendly lady who expressed her view on the few spots of rain we had noticed with a look that said, more eloquently than words: this is Pembrokeshire; what can you expect in winter? She also advised us to keep on through the farmyard, past the polytunnel, to find the path to the Wildlife Centre.

After leaving the farmyard through the gate on the far side, you find yourself at a crossing of paths at **3** (SN1891 4400). Two routes are signposted here to the Centre. One is labelled the 'gorge trail', the other the 'woodland trail'. Both will take you to the Wildlife Centre, but the gorge trail is steep and narrow and leads downhill from here. If you agree with us that steep and narrow paths are (apart from the puff element) best taken uphill, turn left here to follow the woodland trail and leave the gorge trail for the way back.

After a short while, the Woodland trail zig-zags down to a path which runs by the old railway line that ran south from Cardigan to Whitland. The line opened in 1873 to serve the slate quarries in mid-Pembrokeshire (you will come across one of these quarries later on this walk). The line closed in 1963 and is now tarmacked over and used as the drive to the Wildlife Centre. While we were looking over to our left to try and spot the course of the old railway line, we met a chap talking, in an official sort of way, on his mobile phone. When he had finished on his phone, he was quite happy to talk to us instead. He works for Pembrokeshire County Council and told us that he 'walks for his job', checking on the

state of the footpaths, we gathered. This seemed a good opportunity to raise the state of the footpath that is marked on the OS map as following the course of the river. That is when we learned that it had been closed  for some time. Our friend was worried about the fiscal statement from the government which was due the next day. 'Bound to be cuts for Councils', he said. He had just had a pay rise, though, so that cheered him up. The path wanders gently and pleasantly under trees towards the Wildlife Centre. There are a couple of turnings, one to the left and one to the right, which you should ignore. Towards the end you have good views across flat land towards Cardigan.

The Welsh Wildlife Centre at Teifi Marshes was established in 1993 and is owned and managed by the Wildlife Trust of South and West Wales. The reserve covers 264 acres and it would be easy to spend several hours exploring it. The Trust have laid boardwalks across the marshes and there are hides where you can sit and look out for birds and other animals. There are also pieces of industrial archaeology. Near the centre car park, which sits on the former railway line to Cardigan, we came across an old fireplace made of bricks with a piece of railway track as a lintel. The centre building, called the 'Glasshouse' has won architectural awards. It houses a shop and café and toilets and this is a good place to stop for a break. When you are set to continue, follow the sign in front of the centre for the gorge walk.

Take the lane past the holiday accommodation and playground to the signpost for the gorge walk, where you turn right. The river, on the day of our visit, was in full spate, churning brown and fearsomely to the sea. This section of the walk, with the river on your left and old oak trees on the right, is especially pleasant. Soon you come to some slate quarries with an information board giving the history of quarrying here. The old, open quarries are certainly atmospheric places to step into, home (the board tells us) to bats

and peregrine falcons.

There are plenty of reminders of the quarrying in the blocks of slate lying on the path as it continues along the river from here through holly and oak trees. There is a viewing platform at **4** (1917 4496) and a sign warning of the difficulties (but also the beauties) of the path ahead. As the river curves to the right in the next section of the walk, the steep sides of the gorge reach the river bank in a number of places. When this happens, the path heads a little inland, first climbing up steps and then back down steps to the river. This happens several times and your knees will remember this part of the walk for some days. We were on this path at a time when the NHS was in crisis with long waits for A and E and we were careful not to sprain an ankle or break a leg on the steep descents.

Along one of the dips, where the path re-joins the river, we met a fellow walker who told us that he had canoed down this section. When he did it, the river level was lower and he had paddled between boulders which were, on this day, covered with water.

At **5** (1935 4448) take another set of steps immediately up

to the right. The sign for this turning had fallen to the ground on the day of our visit. If you miss the turning and carry on, the path soon peters out. This is the most beautiful and remote part of the walk. The path is narrow in places and it can get muddy and slippy. At one place there is a bit of a scramble over rocks, but it is certainly easier going up than coming down.

The path brings you back to the crossing at **3**, where you can carry on through the farmyard to return the way you came, or turn left to walk through woods back to Cilgerran. We asked a lady that we met here which was the quickest way. 'They are about the same', she said, so we took the turning to the left for variety and were glad that we had done so. There is a steep descent to start with. The path is narrow in places and you have to take care, but this is a fine bit of walking. An information board in these woods tells that Coedmor, the name of the woodland, is an 'ancient woodland clinging to the steep sides of the gorge'. There is a series of footbridges crossing small streams tumbling down towards the river. After the first of these, the path winds through young sycamore and oak trees, but later it takes you into tall pine trees. After several footbridges, the path curves to the right, still under pines, with an open field to the left. We joined a short boardwalk, ducked under a fallen pine tree and passed through a gate into an open field. The path follows the edge of the field to emerge, at **6** (1914 4320) onto the lane in Cilgerran. Turn left here and follow your tracks back to the car park.

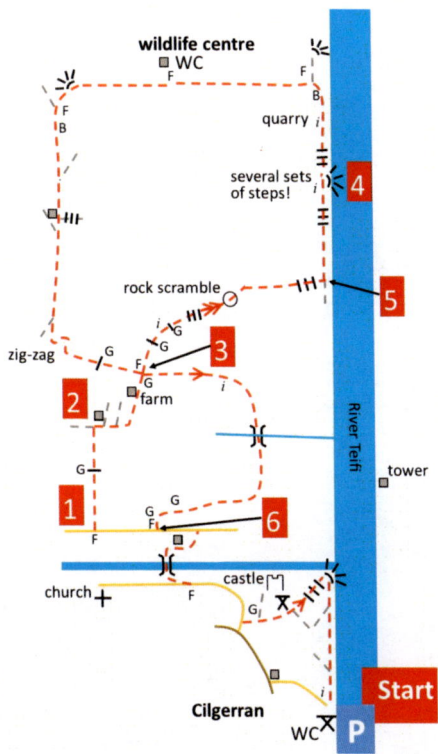

After the walk, the

owner of the village shop in Cilgerran will give you a warm welcome. Her shop sells the usual things but also has a 'zero waste' section, where you can buy basics without the plastic wrappers. You can have a conversation in English or Welsh. If you like your pubs to be traditional, with good beer and conversation, you will enjoy a trip to the Mason's Arms (known locally as Y Rampin) a short distance down the main street to the south of the shop.

Beech

Beech grows strong and tall. It can be found in Pembrokeshire woodlands as single trees sharing space with oak and the other regulars and it can be found, occasionally, in a managed plantation (for example at Stackpole). Beech plantations are shady with a ground cover of orange leaves and crunchy beech nuts. According to the Woodland Trust, only specialist, shade-tolerant plants can survive in a beech forest. Look out for the oval leaves, pointed at the tip and with *wavy* edges. The young leaves are bright green with soft hairs; as they age the leaves become darker and lose their hairs. A good time to be sure of your identification is in the Autumn when the leaves are starting to turn yellow and the beech nuts have formed. The leaves often stay on the tree in winter, turning brown or golden orange. The nuts are easily identified: they are like two small coconut shells fitted together with hairs growing on the outside. Beech nuts are edible. Traditionally they were fed to pigs and they can be roasted and used as a coffee substitute.

Walk 6 Pontfaen

A walk up and down a beautiful river valley, on woodland paths and a country lane. Some steep climbs. Distance 6.5 km. Allow two and a half hours.

The waterfall at the top end of this walk is special because, like Niagara Falls, it comes with its own viewing platform. The waterfall is best seen after plenty of rain; it can be just a trickle on a dry day. It is therefore probably best to reserve this walk for a fine winter's day following rain. The viewing platform is provided by the friends of the National Park. It has a bench, making it a perfect spot for a picnic while you watch and listen to the tumbling water. It's a good idea to take something waterproof to put on the bench to sit on. The walk from Pontfaen is through traditional woodland for nearly all of the way. There is a steady climb up to the waterfall and the going can get muddy when wet. There is a quicker and less muddy return route which you may prefer; choosing that gives you the opportunity to stop at a very special pub.

Take the only path leading from the car park at **1** (SN 0246 3397) eastwards along the south bank of the River Gwaun. A map provided by the National Park (who manage these woods) shows the first part of this walk. Enjoy the walk along the mulchy path with the river on the left and the hillside rising steeply to your right. There are views across the river to the scattered buildings of Pontfaen: the pub, the chapel, the school and a few cottages. The trees we recognised here were beech, oak, birch and holly. Even in winter there is still plenty of colour provided by the bright green

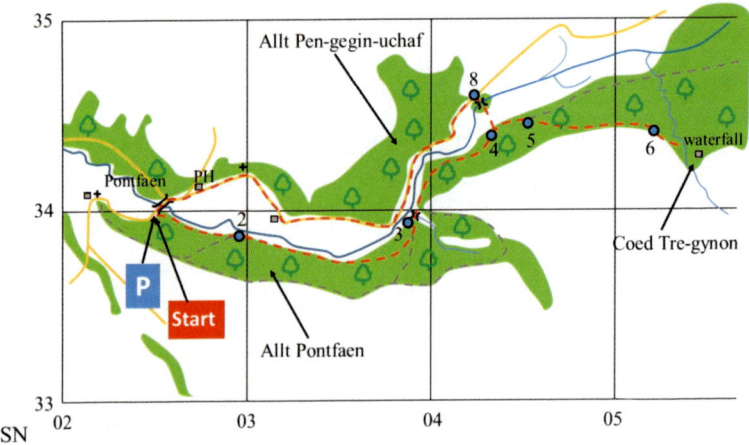

holly bushes and golden beech. Keep left at **2** (0295 3383). Soon afterwards, the river gets close and sure enough, the water-loving Alder with its collection of catkins joins the trees along the river bank. If you are doing this walk after rain, the going gets muddy about now and there are sliced stepping-logs laid here to ease your journey.

The path now leaves the river and you plunge deeper into the woods. There are fallen branches here and it can get boggy underfoot. In wet weather, a stream crosses the path and makes it very wet. Soon after, the river comes close again and the path now rises to meet a signposted junction with a path leading off to the right. Don't take this path but carry on down the steep steps with a wobbly handrail. There is a

tricky junction to negotiate here. Skirt around the prominent building (called Dan Coed), bear off to the right at the gate and cross the bridge over the stream at **3** (0378 3398). Take the path that leads left from the far side of the bridge and then take the bridleway leading away from the water. After about 20 yards, where the bridleway bends to the right and heads up hill, go through the gate in front of you and take the footpath that follows the river bank.

The path here is narrower than it has been on the first part of this walk and it rises and falls as it takes you inland by the side of the meandering stream. At **4** (SN 0430 3453) there is a junction with a path leading off to the left. This is a short-cut home should you choose it on the way back from the waterfall. For now, keep on and take the right fork at **5** (0440 3456) following the path that heads diagonally up the slope away from the river. The soil underfoot alternates between its usual dark brown and a lighter brown like milky coffee. We wondered if the soil colour changes with the amount of leaf mulch it gets from the trees above. This part of the wood, in winter, is remarkable for the number of large, isolated, holly trees. The branches of the holly reach out straight and horizontal from the trunk. Some of the trees are big enough to stand under. This seems to be the time for holly to thrive, when the bigger deciduous trees have undressed for winter, leaving plenty of light and space for their smaller evergreen neighbours.

The climb here makes its demands on your lungs and you will probably find you want to stop from time to time in the places where there is a good view of the valley down to your left. The valley here is wide and flat bottomed with just a small stream meandering its way to the sea. We figured there must be a geological explanation for this wide, steep-sided shape. According to an article in the Welsh Geological Quarterly, available online, the valley was formed by the rushing meltwaters of the warming glaciers at the end of the last ice age. As the glaciers melted, great volumes of water flowed along here to the Irish Sea, underneath the melting ice, carving out a channel 150 feet deep, one-third of a mile wide and with side slopes as steep as 35 degrees. It is up one of these sides that you are climbing now. Geologists consider this to be one of the best examples of a meltwater valley in Britain.

Thankfully, the steep climb eventually levels off and the path takes you along the edge of the woods with an open field on your right. There is the sense of ancient woodland here; moss clings to boulders in the same way as it does in Ty Canol woods (walk 7). At one point a tree stands right in the middle of the path and you can pass it to the left or right. The path then bends to the right and you can hear the sound of the waterfall which is our goal. Go through the gate at **6** (0524 3457) and then climb down the steps to the left. There are 48 steps to go down and then a few to climb up again as you follow the boardwalk to the waterfall at **7**. The inscription on the bench at the viewing platform reads:

Donated by Tregynon in 2019 to the Friends of the PCNP who, with the NPA, restored this permissive path.

When you have enjoyed this lovely place, retrace your steps to **4**. From here, you have three possible routes and the choice will depend on how much time you have left and your energy levels. One is to return the way you came, along the south bank of the river. Another is to walk to the bridge at **3**, climb the steps with the rickety handrail and then take the high-level path marked on the map back to the car park. The third option, and the one we chose, is to go through the gate here, cross the field (which is boggy in winter) and take some more stepping-logs into a small stand of trees through which the stream flows. Cross the stream by the footbridge and go through the gate onto the lane at **8**. Turn left and walk back along this lane. As you walk back you can look across the river to your left to the woods that you have recently traversed. Follow the lane through the spreadeagled hamlet of Pontfaen, past the school, the chapel and the pub – the Dyffryn Arms at **9** - and over the two-arched stone bridge back to the car park.

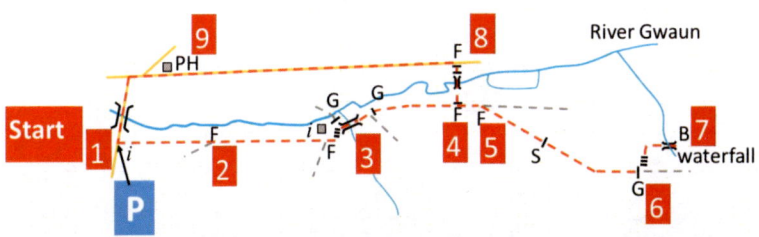

On the afternoon of our walk, in late November, there was a mist in the valley. Cold air, laden with water vapour, was creeping along the river, heading inland. The higher density of the cold air, compared to the warmer air above and to the sides, kept it in the very bottom of the valley. The leading edge of this air current, where it pushed against the slightly warmer air in front, curled back on itself, so that the head of the current was noticeably thicker than the main body that followed. As we watched, this head of mist advanced slowly up the valley, pushed by the pressure of cold air behind. As the sun dropped below the hillside, we were watching two rivers in the valley, one a flow of water heading quickly to sea and the other a flow of cold air, laden with mist, travelling much more slowly inland over the surface of the water. This, together with the waterfall, was the second great performance that nature had put on for us today.

Of course, you don't have to walk past the Dyffryn Arms; you can go inside to quench your thirst. Bessie's, as it is known locally

(after its venerable landlady), is probably the most famous pub in Pembrokeshire and one of the best-known in Wales. Its charm lies in its unchanging nature. This is how pubs used to be and rarely are today. Inside, there is one small room with tables and chairs and customers who talk to each other. Conversation is the main form of entertainment here, often in Welsh and always inclusive. You will be drawn into the story-swopping if you want to be. Beer (draft Bass) is served straight from the barrel into a jug, poured into a glass and passed through a hatch. Having a pint at Bessie's is a special experience and long may it remain so.

Holly

Everyone knows the holly. The prickly, shiny green leaves and bright red berries have featured on Christmas Cards since cards were first exchanged. Not so familiar is the bark: it has a light brown, coppery colour and is covered in many little 'warts'. The branches are very straight and make excellent walking sticks. In J.K. Rowling's Harry Potter books, holly is the favoured wood for making magic wands.

Holly is native to the UK and there

are many varieties available for the garden. The natural woodland holly, Ilex aquifolium, can grow up to 15 metres and live for 300 years. The trees that we saw in the wild grew close to, and in the shade of, larger deciduous trees. They come into their own in winter when their green leaves and red berries stand out.

Gwaun Valley New Year

In Pembrokeshire's Gwaun Valley there is a tradition of celebrating the start of the new year on the 13th of January (or perhaps on the nearest Saturday). Children visit friends' houses to sing songs and parties are held in Community centres.

This tradition, Hen Galan in Welsh, has its roots in the old Julian Calendar, which was the official calendar in Britain until 1752. The Julian calendar was established by the Romans and had a leap year of 366 days every four years. This works if there are exactly 365.25 days in the year but in fact there are 365.24 days. This small error in counting the days accumulated over the centuries until we adopted the Gregorian calendar which had a better way of counting leap years. To bring us in line with other countries that already used the new calendar, 12 days were omitted from the year 1752. Not everyone accepted this change straight away. The new year in the Gwaun Valley harks back to the old way of counting the days.

Walk 7 — Tŷ Canol woods

A circular walk of about 6.5 km. Mostly on the level, on bridleways and mulchy paths, through one of the finest stretches of ancient oak woodland in the country. Allow 2.5 hours.

Tŷ Canol is a National Nature Reserve. It's ancient oak trees and moss-covered boulders have an other-worldly feel. This is what home must have been like for our ancestors, we can imagine, five thousand years ago. Part of the  atmosphere of Tŷ Canol is no doubt due to its isolation. There are few houses nearby and no busy road. 'It's so quiet here', one fellow walker said.

This walk to Tŷ Canol takes you through two other woodlands, Pentre Ifan and Hagr y Coed, which are also charming. The going is mostly flat but it can get muddy in places after rain. Another hazard, we found, is that it is quite easy to get lost. The central parts of the woods all look similar and it is possible to take a wrong

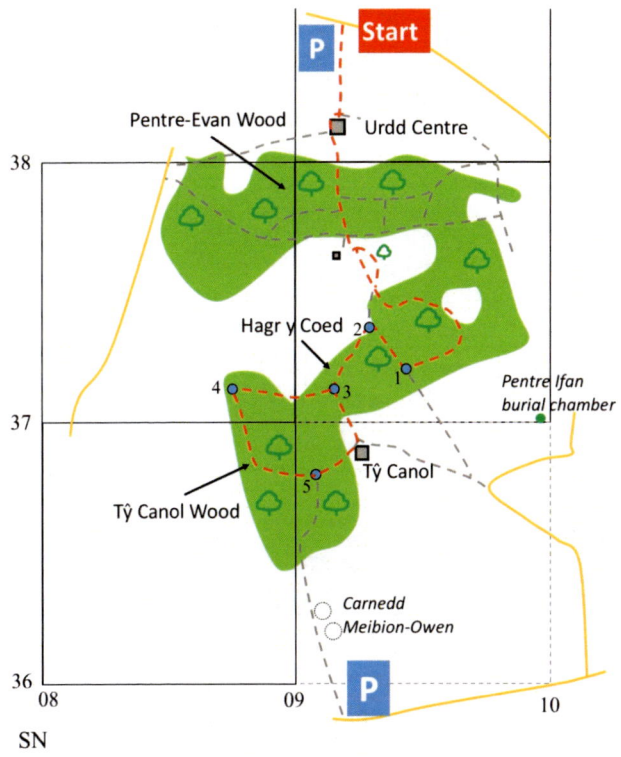

turning without realising. It doesn't help that the woods are located right on a fold of the OS Explorer map. This is a good walk to take a compass along for the journey.

The walk begins on the lane leading down to the Pentre Ifan Urdd centre (SN 093 383). There is limited parking at the top of the lane (the centre itself is private) where there are views to the impressive Carningli mountain over the hedge to the west. Walk down the concrete path to the Urdd centre, passing the centre buildings on your left. You soon enter the woods. The information board tells us that this first part of the walk, Pentre Ifan woods, is managed by the National Park Authority. This part of the woods dates back to the 12th century. In the 1960's, it was planted with conifers, but these have now mostly gone and native deciduous trees, mostly oak, have re-established themselves. There is a network of paths in Pentre Ifan woods and it would be pleasant to spend an hour or two here, but our destination lies ahead.

Soon after entering the woods, the path goes through a small stream. You can either splash your way through this or take the simple stone bridge on the side. At the fork, bear right to follow the path towards Tŷ Canol woods. The path is broad here; it is a bridleway. Near the path are shrubs and small trees (we recognised sycamore, holly and hawthorn) with larger trees further back. A cuckoo was calling in the woods. Soon after this, we met a walker with two dogs. 'Did you hear the cuckoo' she said. 'It's the first time I've heard it this year'.

At the wooden sign put up by NRW noting 'Coed Tŷ Canol in 35m' turn left off the bridleway and then almost immediately right through the gate. The information board here tells us that these woods were 'already old when Pentre Ifan stone burial chamber was built 5500 years ago.' You have a choice of walking up what

looks like a drover's track between banks and hedgerows (that lies straight ahead) or striking off to the left through more open country. Both routes bring you to the same point where (at the time of our visit) a noticeboard says that the path ahead is closed and asks you to take the diversion off to the left. Although this takes you off a direct route to the main Tŷ Canol woods, it is worth it. After a short walk through woodland and a crossing, by stepping-stones, of a small stream, the path tales you to a large open meadow with isolated trees. In spring and summer there is a carpet of soft grass and flowers. This is a pleasant interlude between the two main pieces of woodland on this walk.

The path re-enters the cover of trees by a noticeboard and a lovely old spreading oak tree with its branches arched over to touch the ground. The noticeboard explains why trees are being felled to allow the mosses and lichens to get enough light. Walk up the path leading from the meadow and you come to the ancient woodland and see what it is famous for. Old twisted oak trees can be seen in every direction and, between them, lie lichen-covered boulders. Sunlight filtering through the tree canopy gives the floor a dappled appearance. The oak is king here. The leaf mould under your feet is made of their brown leaves and young oak shoots, just a few inches high, appear out of tiny grassy spaces.

At the T-junction **1** (SN 0953 3724), turn right. You are now on the upper end of the path on which we passed the closed sign earlier. Keep your eye out for a junction on the left leading to a gate and when you reach it (at **2** SN 0930 3735), turn down this path and pass through the gate. On the map, this seems to be the transition from Hagr y Coed to Tŷ Canol wood, but it is difficult to see any difference on the ground. Follow the path across a small stream, noting the views of Carningli across the open field to your right. There is another gate, set to the side of the path and then a step across a small stream before the path arrives at a T-junction (**3** SN 0921 3717) which is the start of our circular walk around Tŷ Canol woods.

You can turn either way at this junction. We turned right and followed the path which bends left and took the left fork under the branches of a spreading oak tree. The path twists and turns quite a lot here as it passes through a rocky outcrop. This is a lovely old part of the wood. Soon the path brings you back to the open field, separated here from the path by a double gate. Blue arrow posts have been put here to show the way but the path is also  pretty well trodden. Cross the boardwalk and you will shortly reach the corner of the woods (at **4**, where there is a map and a stile leading out of the woods.

Your route bends left here, continuing through the woods. The path climbs gently and there is a gully down to your left. Follow the path, which is now quite narrow but well-marked up to a T-junction (**5** SN 0912 3683) and here turn left up towards a clearing.

Walk up to the gate leading to Tŷ Canol house, past the NRW map and then turn left down the marked footpath leading into the wood. Follow the broad path down to junction **3**. Turn right here and make your way back to the car park the way you came.

After the walk, it would be a shame not to visit Pentre Ifan burial chamber while you are so close. According to Cadw, who manage and care for this site, the stone framework, once covered in a grassy mound, is constructed from 'bluestones' from the nearby Preseli Hills (Stonehenge in Wiltshire also contains many of these bluestones). Pentre Ifan was constructed over 5,000 years ago during the Neolithic or new stone age period. This was a time when stone tools still predominated but people had moved on from foraging to farming.

Clock of Ages

If, like us, you struggle to place the bronze age in its historical context and are unsure exactly when the medieval period was, you might find this picture helpful. The lifetime of the British Isles, as we would recognise them, has been divided into the 12 hours of the clockface. The islands reached

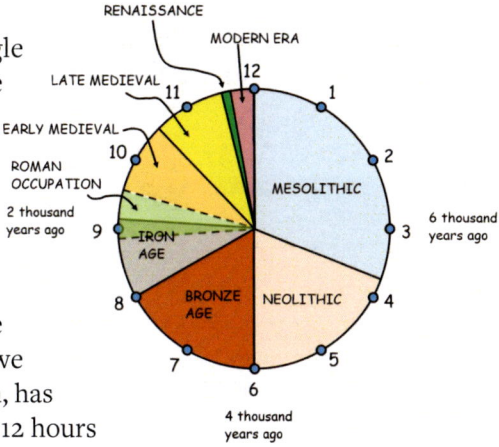

their present shape at the end of the last ice age about 8,000 years ago and that is represented by 12 noon on the clock. The present time is represented by midnight and so 8,000 years of history is condensed into 12 hours at the rate of 670 years per hour. Some important periods in our history are marked. There is some uncertainty in the exact dates of some of these: the bronze age and the end of the Mesolithic for example. They probably started and ended at different times in different parts of the islands, so it is perhaps best to imagine blurred boundaries between them rather than the sharp lines we have drawn.

Some of the principal events in our history fit in as follows. The Pentre Ifan burial site in Pembrokeshire dates from about 5,500 years ago, during the neolithic and appeared at about 4.30pm on our clock. The nearby woods at Tŷ Canol were already in existence at that time. The Norman Invasion of England in 1066 would be placed at 10.30 (at the end of the early medieval) and the Industrial Revolution in Britain, which began the 'modern age', would have been at 20 to midnight.

Remarkably, the oldest living trees in Wales were young saplings at about 5pm on our clock. They have been around for most of our history.

Oak

Oaks are wonderful trees. Strong, good-looking and useful. They are readily identified by their leaves which have 4 or 5 rounded lobes on either side. Their fruits – acorns - are also easy to spot in the Autumn. Oaks produce hard, durable timber, prized for furniture and house-building. It is also a great wood for ship-building: Nelson's fleet at Trafalgar was constructed of oak (although not all from British oak, a lot of Swedish trees were imported for that job). The tannin in oak bark has been used in leatherwork since Roman times. Oak trees support more wildlife – birds, small mammals and insects - than any other kind of native woodland.

There are many varieties of oak tree worldwide but only two are native to Britain: the common or English oak and the sessile or Welsh oak. The latter is more common on the west coast of Britain. There are differences in the leaves, but the surest way of telling them apart (if you really want to) is by the stalks of the acorns: Welsh oaks have short acorn stalks (sessile means 'without a stalk').

The Welsh word for oak, derwen, features in many place names in Wales (Clunderwen in Pembrokeshire) and across Britain (Derwentwater in the Lake District).

Walk 8 Brandy Brook

Distance 4.5 km for the circuit starting from Roch Bridge. Allow 1.5 hours. Add another 2 kilometres and 50 minutes if starting from the A487.

Brandy Brook is a small stream flowing to the sea at Newgale on St Bride's Bay. Some three kilometres east of Newgale, the brook enters Eweston Wood where it has arrived from its source in the gentle hills that lie inland. The section through the wood makes a charming walk along the banks of the river and past the still recognisable ruins of an old corn mill. The name 'Brandy Brook' is an obscure one; we wondered if it came from the brown colour of the stream in its more industrial past. The water in the stream is clear enough today.

The T11 bus running from St David's to Haverfordwest will drop you at the Victoria Inn at Roch and you take the lane that leads inland from here, past the school. It's about a kilometre along the lane to the start of the footpath at Roch Bridge. If you are driving, there is limited parking (for two small cars) at Roch Bridge. In the woods to the left of the lane before you get to Roch Bridge, the OS map shows the workings of an old colliery. It lies on private land and is inaccessible to the public but it is noteworthy because it lies at the western end of the Pembrokeshire coal field, which runs from St Bride's Bay in the west to the coast between Saundersfoot and Amroth in the east. Coal was mined commercially in Pembrokeshire from the 13th to the 20th century, at dozens of small collieries like this one. The coal was high-grade Anthracite, the best kind of solid fuel: it burns hot with little smoke. The last coal mine in the county closed soon after the second world war, but that wasn't quite the end of the story. M.R. Connop-Price's book 'Pembrokeshire, the forgotten coalfield', tells that when, in 1990, a new primary school was being constructed at Kilgetty, 12 miles to the east of here, coal was discovered on the surface. In just a few weeks, nearly 5,000 tons were extracted by mechanical diggers and sold commercially.

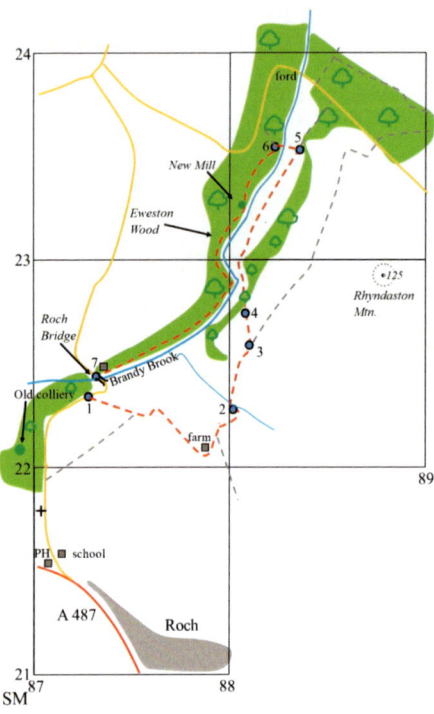

Leave the lane on the farm track at **1** (SM 8731 2230) signposted to Woodhawk. Follow this track, lined with trees and telegraph poles, as it climbs out of the valley. Pass Woodhawk farm on your left and carry on along the grassy path to the gate. Keep to the left edge of the field until you come to another gate in the corner of the field. Follow the path here as it curves left and then right through the trees and then cross the small stream at **2**. Big, bold steps are needed here to make your feet meet the stepping stones! Follow the track up the hill in front of you, through the gorse bushes, to the gate. Keep going up the hill with the fence on your right. Eweston Woods, where we will be later, are down below you to the left.

At the fingerpost at **3** (SM 8812 2259), branch off at an angle to the left, following the contours of

the land across an open field to the gate in the far corner (**4**, SM 8811 2277). Go through this gate and follow the path through the gorse. This is a fine walking path, sloping slightly down at the start and gradually becoming more wooded

as you travel along it. There are good views across the valley to your left. After crossing a stile, a gate leads to an open field. Follow the fence on the left across the open space with the lovely rising hillside off to the right. Look out for the marker post at **5** (SM 8842 2358) and turn left here to cross the Brandy Brook. The handrails on the bridge don't leave much space between.

You are now entering the woodland proper and the best part of the walk. Cross a plank bridge and step over a stream to climb the side of the valley and join a broad path at **6** (SM 883 236). Turn left here; the path climbs above the stream which meanders along in the valley below. There is a rope swing dangling from a tree branch high above the valley. The view is spectacular but the swing itself looks terrifying: the sort of thing parents might want to keep their children well away from. The path crosses an open space before entering the woods again and you come across some prominent

ruins at SM 8809 2328. This is 'New Mill', marked on the Ordnance Survey maps published in 1888. It is an old corn mill, one of several that operated on Brandy Brook. Water-powered mills spread rapidly through Wales in the 14th century and became an important part of the food industry. Farmers brought their grain to the Miller, who ground it into wheat, which was made into bread by the Baker, who then sold loaves to everybody. In this way, the medieval economy went around.

This particular mill was abandoned at some stage in the late 19th or early 20th century, presumably as cheaper, or faster ways of grinding grain into flour became available. Touchingly, though, there are still reminders of the Miller to be found here if you visit at the right time. In the spring, the grounds around the mill are awash with daffodils and snowdrops, presumably planted by the Miller and his family when they lived here. The humans may have departed, but the bulbs they planted are still flourishing and even spreading into the nearby woods.

Continuing the walk downstream, look out for the railway sleepers used in the construction of fence posts here. You can see the holes where the steel chocks which fixed the rails to the sleepers were attached. These sleepers would have carried the 4.15 to Paddington (and many another service) before being pressed into their current job. This part of the walk is a good striding path: mulchy ground beneath your feet, trees all round, birds singing, a tumbling stream and the wind rustling the trees. Great! Follow the path along the stream, sometimes close, sometimes further away, until you reach some buildings and return to the lane at Roch Bridge at 7 (SM 8733 2237).

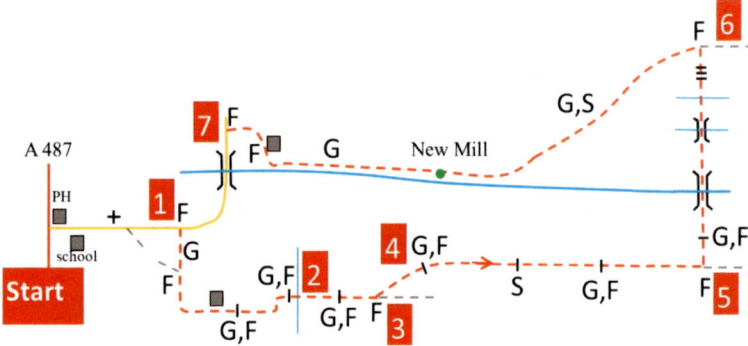

After the walk, you might like to have a look at Newgale, where the Brandy Brook flows into the sea. This is one of the largest beaches in Pembrokeshire; from here there is a clear run out into the Atlantic and large ocean waves run up on to the beach. The wide expanse of sand is backed by a shingle bank. This is a popular spot for water sports. We sat in the car, watching wind surfers coping with a stiff breeze and discussed the two different types of energy we had seen on this walk. Is there more coal in Pembrokeshire? Probably. Possibly lots, although much of it difficult to get at (although not all, as the Kilgetty experience shows). However, given the effect of burning fossil fuels on the environment it is best left where it is. The water mills are a different story. In fact, they are the opposite, aren't they? They became redundant when steam and diesel engines took over the role. Re-instating water power would surely be good for the environment. Can there be a cleaner source of energy than a tumbling stream? Perhaps this time, the power in the flowing water could be used to generate electricity, or synthesise hydrogen.

Elder

We find Elders really useful trees. The flowers can be used for making Elderflower cordial, the berries for making wine and, when the tree dies, the wood makes a good slow-burning and hot fuel for an open fire.

The tree is probably most easily identified by its bark, which is light brown or grey with a deep crevassed surface. The leaves are oval-shaped and pointed with a serrated edge. The flowers appear in the spring. They are white and strongly perfumed. The black berries ripen in the Autumn.

Elders are often found in hedgerows but they also make an appearance as isolated trees in woodland.

The age of trees

A record of a tree's age is kept in the rings within its trunk. It is not necessary to cut the tree down to count its rings – a core can be taken from the trunk without harming it too much. Tree rings are composed of two parts: light and dark coloured. The light part is formed when the tree is growing quickly in the spring and summer and the darker wood is added when the growth slows in the autumn and winter. By counting the rings, you can work out the age of the tree, although this isn't always easy because the rings become hard to identify in places. The rings contain useful information about climate conditions during the tree's lifetime. A particularly broad ring indicates a good year when there was a long growing season. Thin rings tell of poor years for the tree.

The picture shows some rings from a branch of a Scots pine tree, which had been lopped off by the owners and was lying on the ground when we came across it. The branch was about 3 inches, or 8 cm in diameter and we reckoned it was 10 years old. It looks as though in its early life the cross-section was pretty circular and then had become oval in later years.

Trees can live for hundreds or, in some cases, thousands of years and the information in tree rings provides valuable insight to how the climate of our planet has changed during that time. Some of the oldest specimens in the UK are yew trees growing in churchyards. It is possible that some church yews date back several thousand years. Some of the oak trees in Pembrokeshire's Tŷ Canol woods are several hundred years old and would have been saplings at the time of the Spanish armada.

Walk 9 Treffgarne Gorge

A 7.5 km walk with some steep climbs and descents. Allow 3 hours to complete the circuit, more if you want to explore the sights on the way.

This circular walk takes you along both sides of the valley of the western Cleddau where it squeezes through the narrow gorge along with the main road and the railway line leading to Fishguard. The sides of the valley are steep

and rise to the dramatic rock formations of the Treffgarne rocks: familiar sights to anyone who has driven along the A40 between Haverfordwest and Fishguard. We did the walk in a clockwise direction, starting just south of Wolf's Castle, heading south along the wooded eastern side of the valley and then back northwards up the rocky western side. The walk is quite a strenuous one, with some fairly steep climbs. It can also get very wet underfoot where a spring makes the path boggy, so come prepared. The trees are a mixture of deciduous and conifers. There is industrial heritage in the gorge. Isambard Kingdom Brunel planned to build a railway through here in the middle of the 19th century. The railway was never finished but you can still see the remains of the workings.

Parking is available just south of Wolf's Castle on the A40. There are two laybys close together here. Either will do, but the more northerly one (SM 9568 2564) is closer to the start of the walk. Look out for the green fingerpost on the other side of the main road and take care crossing: this is a busy road. The T5 bus running between Fishguard and Haverfordwest will drop you in Wolf's Castle or on the A40 near Treffgarne.

From the fingerpost, follow the steps leading downhill towards the river. Cross the footbridge and head between the fenceposts to the trees standing on the hillside in front of you. Go through the gates and under the railway bridge. The bridge carries the line from Goodwick and Fishguard to Carmarthen and onwards to the world. More of that later. Take the gate to the right and follow the path between fenceposts. Ignore the turning to the left and go through the gate in front to follow the path uphill.

The path here is narrow with a steep drop to the right and steep incline to the left. You soon enter a conifer plantation where the trees grow close together and it can be quite dark on an overcast day. It is not easy to see the path here; if in doubt, keep heading uphill and look out for the fingerpost at **1** (SM 9586 2536). There is a small clearing here before the path continues uphill under the close cover of pines. Bouncy pine needles lie in a thick layer underfoot. We could poke our walking sticks a good six inches into this soft ground cover. You reach an embankment where the path bends to the right to follow the height contours. The path emerges into a clearing with a rock outcrop on your right. There are fine views from the top of this across the gorge to the curious rock formations on the other side.

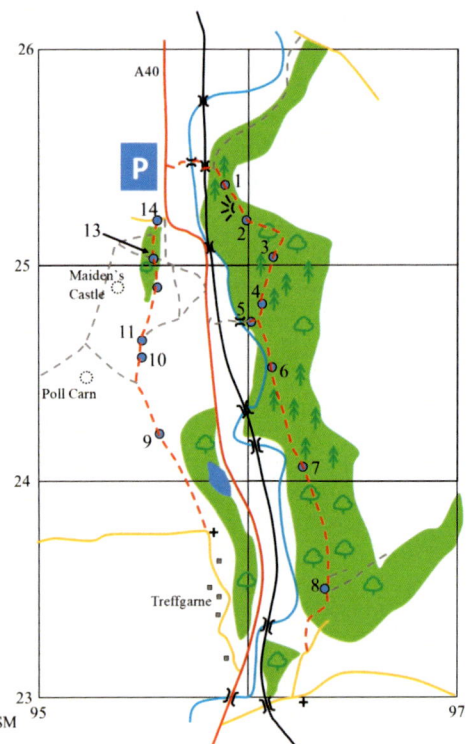

The path continues through deciduous trees to the gap in an old boundary wall at **2** (SM 9595 2521). There are now pines to your right and, over the fence to your left, an open field. Shortly after the communications mast, the path bends to the

right and becomes boggy. There is a spring marked on the OS map and it crosses and floods the path here. A boardwalk has been provided but it is not really up to the job. The bridge crossing the stream at **3** (SM 9612
2503) had collapsed at the time of our visit. We took the stepping stones to the side as the bridge looked unsafe. This is a popular walk in mid-Pembrokeshire but, sadly, this section was not in a good condition on our trips here. Carry on past the turn to the left to a gate which brings you into some very nice mixed woodland. On one visit, it was snowing hard at this point and the trees looked enchanting in their snowy covers.

At **4** (SM 9605 2479) follow the signed path which leads down into the valley. This is a steep descent and we had to hold on to branches in places to make sure we didn't lose our footing. The path continues up the steps on the left at **5** (SM 9600 2472) but you might want to take some time here to look at the old workings which are part of Brunel's attempt to put a railway line through the gorge. In 1851, 54 years before the present line to Fishguard was built, the great Victorian engineer Isambard Kingdom Brunel laid the trackbed for a railway here. The plan was to run a line from Carmarthen to

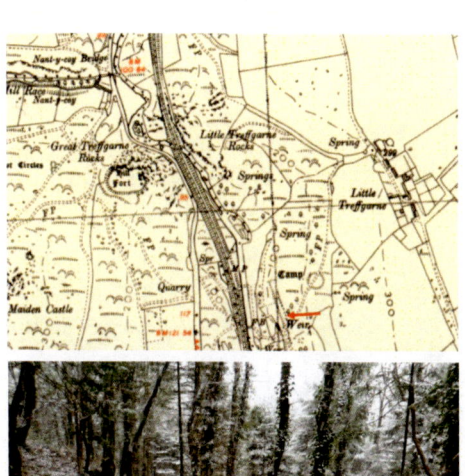

Abermawr near Fishguard. The work was not completed and instead Brunel chose Neyland as the terminus of his line in Pembrokeshire. All that remains of the works now is the tumbled-down stone walls of an old building and an embankment with a trench on the side. The structure is overgrown and hard to see. If we hadn't been told to look out for it, we would have missed it. The large rocks at the base of the embankment have slowed the growth of the trees and this gives a clue to the line that the track followed.

Evidence of the workings is visible on old six-inch to the mile OS maps including the one shown here, which was published in 1953. It must have been quite an engineering challenge to squeeze the railway line into the narrow gap offered by Treffgarne gorge. The present line was completed, by the Great Western Railway, in 1905. In its short journey through the gorge it crosses from one side of the river and back again 5 times in a distance of about three kilometres. The engineers have gone to great trouble to make the line as straight as possible, to give a smooth and fast ride. It is not just the designers that can take a pride in this line. When you come up close to the railway structures, such as a bridge over the path, you can see the fine craftmanship in the brickwork. Someone has taken trouble over the details of construction even though it would

never be seen by passengers travelling on the line above. The bricks have been laid in what our DIY book tells us is an English bond: a layer of bricks with their broadside facing you alternating with a layer of bricks showing their narrow end.

When the line was in its heyday in the first half of the 20th century, with passing locomotives filling the gorge with steam, passengers could join the trains and alight at a number of 'halts' that are no longer operating. It took just over 20 minutes to travel from Clarbeston Road to Mathry Road, as a timetable published in 1949 shows.

Clarbeston Road	9.50
Wolf's Castle Halt	10.02
Welsh Hook Halt	10.06
Mathry Road	10.11

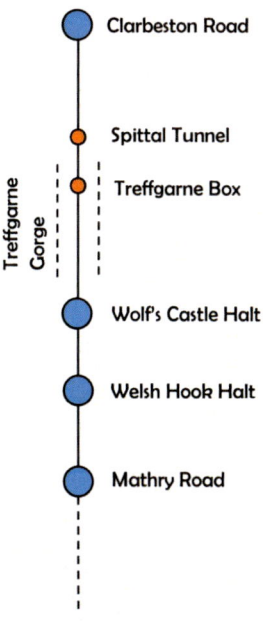

Leave **5** by the steps and follow the narrow mulchy path through the mixed woodland. The ground slopes up to the left and down to the right and the path climbs, not very distinctly, diagonally upwards. At the top, the path becomes broader and there is an open field to the left. You enter a pine wood at **6** (SM 9608 2449). This is a good, level, striding path; a place to use up energy at a brisk walking pace and make quick progress. You are travelling along a shoulder in the topography, a steep slope down into the valley on your right and more gently rising ground to your left. The path emerges from the conifers at a stile at **7** (SM 9626 2406) into mixed woodland. There are some fine holly trees along here. At one point, the path passes under them so that they form an arch overhead: a 'hollytunnel'! This is one of the best parts of the walk: a lovely mulchy path with oak and beech; fast walking over level ground.

The path ends at a gate at **8** (SM 9636 2358) where you turn right to join a bridleway leading downhill. The track here is of the sort often laid by farmers: strips of concrete either side of a middle track of grass. Cross a stream and join the tarmac lane which leads, through the fine tunnel, to the A40.

To continue the circuit, turn right on to the main road and walk along the pavement by the side of the A40 for about 100 yards, cross the road and take the turning signposted Treffgarne. Follow the lane as it twists its way uphill through the straggling houses of the village until you reach the church where the lane bends away to the left. Leave the lane here and follow the concreted bridle path. Keep left at **9** (SM 9560 2421) following the

bridleway. We were joined at this point by a friendly dog who came with us to the open field where we met a little group of donkeys who looked as though they were hoping we had brought some food. Skirt around the right-hand side of the field, which has its own small rocky outcrops. There are two larger stone outcrops visible here. The one in front is called Maiden's Castle and the one off to the left is Poll Carn. Both are popular with rock climbers and are the remains of ancient volcanoes which were active about 600 million years ago.

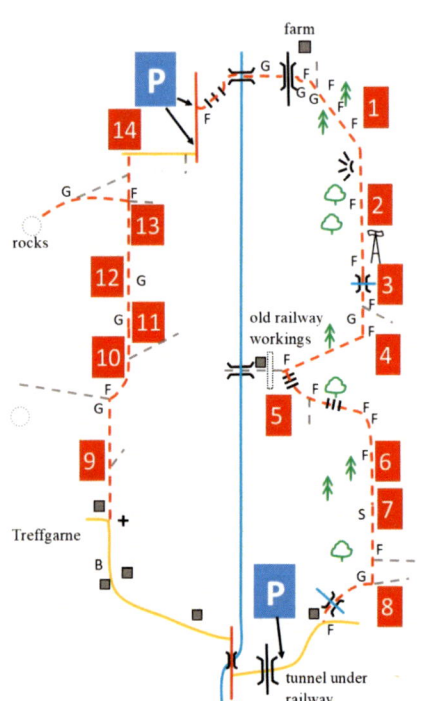

Keep to the right of the field (passing a gate with an arrow at **10** (SM 9555 2460)) to emerge at the corner **11** (SM 9554 2466) onto a path that leads through ferns and gorse bushes. There are young oak and birch trees here. If these are left to grow they will make a good woodland in the future. Go through the gate at **12** (SM

9559 2492) to the crossing of paths at **13** (SM 9560 2506). Turning left here will take you to Maiden's Castle. These rocks really are eye-catching and there are panoramic views from there. Continuing straight ahead at **13** the path brings you out on to a lane at **14** (SM 9555 2520). Turn right and walk down the steep hill to the A40. A short walk along the pavement here will bring you back to the layby on the way to Wolf's Castle.

After the walk, there is an interesting country park to explore at Scolton Manor. The manor and its grounds can be reached by driving along the lane through the Treffgarne tunnel and carrying on through the village of Spittal. The manor is owned and managed by Pembrokeshire County Council and is well used for all sorts of activities. One reason for choosing it to accompany this walk is that there is a 'railway garden' in which, amongst other exhibits, you can find the old station adverts we picture here and a reconstruction of a signal box similar to the one that used to stand in Treffgarne Gorge. We did notice, though, that the brickwork was not laid with an English bond and wondered if the reconstructors had missed a trick. There is an excellent tea room on the site which serves hot meals and tea in earthenware pots with china cups and saucers. Just how it should be!

Hazel

Hazel is most easily identified in the spring and summer by its nuts, which are familiar to anyone who has read children's books about squirrels. The leaves are quite round, pointed at the tip and serrated around the edge. Catkins appear before the leaves and hang in clusters.

Walk 10 Pickle Wood

8 kilometres on a straight level path. You should do it in less than 3 hours.

This walk takes you along the north shore of the Eastern Cleddau River. The path is a good one and the slopes are gentle. This is a good walk to stretch your legs and burn off some calories and, because it is impossible to get lost, you can let your mind wander as you walk and set the world to rights.

The main part of the path is straightforward (and straight), at first through the charmingly named Pickle Wood and later through Warren Wood. Glimpses of the river can be seen between the trees and there are buildings of historical interest at each end of the walk. When we first did this walk, it was possible to park on the lane outside Blackpool Mill, a 19th century water-powered flour mill (built on the site of a former ironworks). The mill was undergoing renovations, though and parking on the lane here may not be an option for long. There is a public car park a short distance from the mill at SN 0583 1427. Walk back to the mill and take the bridleway at **1** (SN 0609 1441).

The bridleway takes you down the side of the mill to the handsome single-spanned and arched bridge. This is a good place to meet fellow walkers who stop to look over the parapet at the water. A group of fish had caught one couple's attention. 'Look at these', said the man, and indeed they were fascinating. 'Coy carp', pronounced our friend, 'they must have escaped into the river and turned wild'. Their surroundings seem to suit them, they looked fat

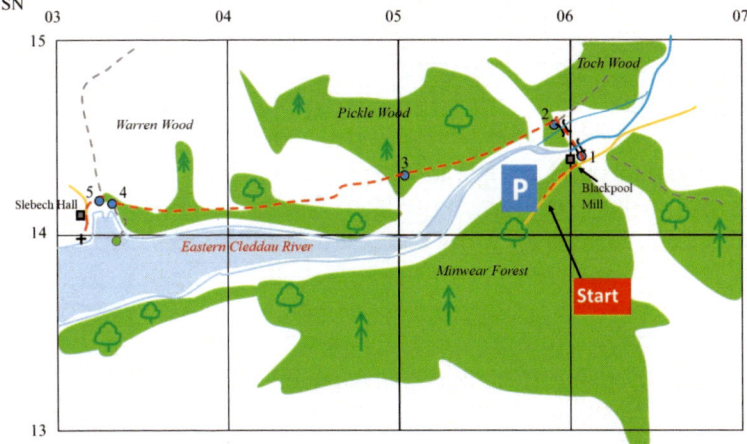

and healthy. Another walker told us that this is a good place to spot kingfishers, although he thought the work on the mill might have put them off as he hadn't seen any for a while.

The sign at the top of the bridge, carved into a stone, reads:

```
BLACKPOOL BRIDGE
ERECTED ABOUT THE YEAR 1830
BARONESS DE RUTZEN
THEN OWNER OF THE SLEBECH ESTATE
RESIDENCE SLEBECH HALL
```

The fact that the year is recorded as 'about' 1830 struck us as strange. Perhaps the plaque was added some years after the bridge was finished.

Continuing on the bridleway, you soon cross a smaller bridge over a brook at **2** (SN 0590 14544). This bridge also bears a date (1987), harder to spot and possibly a time of renovation rather than construction (the bridge looked much older than that to us).

Cross the bridge and turn left at the T-junction. The path here is stony and level. This is a path for fast walking, initially through pine trees on the left and deciduous trees on the right. The path is very straight here; we wondered if the Baroness herself used to ride along it, perhaps to see her bridge being built. After a while you pass a small pond on the right and reach a gate at **3** (SN 0502 1433) bearing a sign for 'Slebech Park Restaurant and Rooms'. The sign also advertises teas and ices available at the restaurant. As there are no cars along here, we wondered if this was meant to entice walkers and if the restaurant welcomed walking boots. More on that later.

Continue on the path, which slopes gently downhill and gets closer to the river. The melodious sound of song birds in the trees is joined by the honking of river birds. There are rhododendron bushes growing along the side of the path here, a sign that this used to be the approach to a stately home. Eventually, you catch sight of Slebech Hall, situated in prime position on the edge of the river.

At **4** (SN 0334 1411) there is a path down to the left which takes you to an island on which the OS map marks a ruined church and which is now home to a small cemetery for pets. Continuing on the main path to **5** (SN 03324 1416) brings you to the lane leading to Slebech Hall. This fine set of buildings is now a hotel. Turn left at the pond in which the water level is controlled by a sluice gate. The lane up to the hotel is private but there is a public footpath to the old church, now a ruin, which lies behind the hotel. As we walked around the church we came across a metal plaque placed by the '1805 club', a charity founded in 1990 for the care and preservation of memorials associated with the navy of the Georgian era. The plaque told us that the church houses the mortal remains of Sir William and Lady Catherine Hamilton. Sir William was a diplomat who married Catherine Barlow of Slebech in 1758. Their marriage was a happy one; they shared a love of music. Lady Catherine died in 1782 and Sir William married Emma Hart who became Lady Emma Hamilton and had a notorious affair with Lord Nelson. When Sir William died, he asked for his body to be returned to Pembrokeshire and buried alongside Lady Catherine in the church here.

In mediaeval times, this area was an important meeting place for pilgrims on their way to and from the cathedral at St. David's. After the Norman Conquest, it became a base for the Knights Hospitaller of St John who supported crusades and pilgrimages to the Holy Land. When Henry VIII oversaw the end of the monasteries, the land was given to the Barlow family who built Slebech Hall in 1750. The hall passed through various hands, ending in the 1830's with the De Rutzen family, the Barons of Slebech. The first Baron invested in the estate, building the large church nearby on the A40 and the bridge at Blackpool Mill. The house remained the property of the family until 1944 when Major John De Rutzen was killed in action in Italy.

We heard Canada Geese honking as they drifted down the river, which is tidal here and flows between mud banks at low tide. There is an old chart in the museum at Milford Haven which appears to show a crossing of the river here. The chart is undated but has the appearance of the late 1700's. Any crossing at this point would have been restricted by the state of the tide. It would have been much safer to cross by the bridge at Blackpool Mill which was probably built at the first practicable crossing place. Still, we noticed footprints in the mud here, proving that some people are still brave enough to make the crossing!

The hotel does have a café and restaurant with tables outside which make a fine place for walkers to sit and rest. There is even a spot where you can clean your boots and wash your dog's paws if necessary! Check the hotel's website for opening times.

When you are ready, head back to Blackpool Mill the way you came.

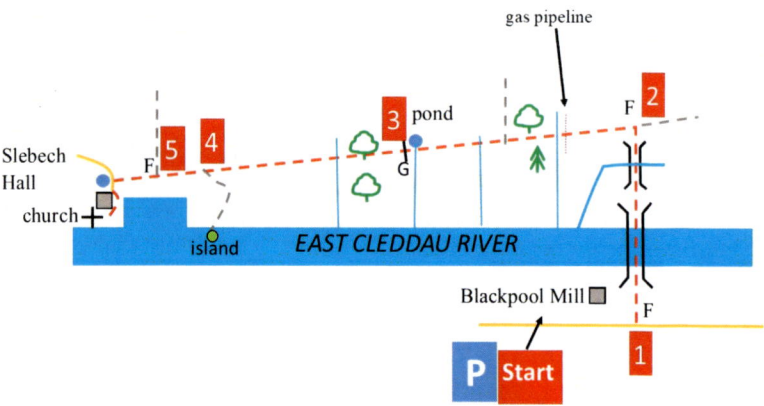

Horse Chestnut

You might think that horse chestnut trees are a little too fancy to be native to Britain and you would be right. According to the Woodland Trust, these trees were first brought to this country from Turkey in the late 16th century. The trees are majestic, with five-lobed leaves like a large hand, and conkers which fall to the ground in the Autumn, just in time for the new school term.

Horse chestnuts hold a special place in the history of this country. During the Great War of 1914-1918, Britain was running out of the chemicals it needed to make cordite, an explosive used in munitions. The necessary ingredients could be manufactured from the starch found in conkers and acorns. In the Autumn of 1917, a call went out to schoolchildren and scouts to collect conkers for the war effort. The reward was seven shillings and sixpence for every hundredweight sent in.

Oxygen Factories

Trees, like all living things, contain carbon (among other elements). Humans get their carbon from the food they eat. Trees obtain their carbon from carbon dioxide gas in the atmosphere. When you look at a tree, you are seeing a structure made from solidified air.

About one-half of a tree's dry weight is carbon. Carbon dioxide is heavier than the carbon it contains – about 3.7 times heavier. So, take a tree's weight, multiply by ½ and then by 3.7 and that's the mass of CO_2 needed to make the tree. An oak tree weighing 10 tonnes has taken up, or 'sequestered' about 10 x ½ x 3.7, or 18 tonnes of carbon dioxide. That's more carbon dioxide than the weight of the tree! The excess mass is given off as oxygen in photosynthesis.

Let's say our oak tree grows by 5% each year. It will produce 500kg of new wood per annum of which about 250kg is carbon. In the process of photosynthesis, the tree strips the oxygen from the carbon dioxide and releases that back into the atmosphere. For each kilogram of carbon absorbed by the tree, 2.7 kg of oxygen is released, so our tree puts about 670kg of oxygen into the atmosphere each year. Without trees and other photosynthetic plants, we would not be here.

A human breathes about 9.5 tonnes of air in a year, but oxygen only makes up about one-quarter of that by mass, and we extract only about 1/3 of the oxygen in each breath. That works out at about 700kg of oxygen per person per year. One good-sized oak tree can provide an individual's oxygen needs.

Walk 11   Canaston Woods

A circular walk of 5 km. Mostly level on bridleways and grassy paths. Allow 2 hours.

Canaston is a mixed woodland, with tall pine trees in the interior and broadleaf trees and bushes growing close to the path. It is bisected by the Knight's Way, a waymarked route which begins in the south-east of the county, but the real glory of these woods lies in the small paths that take you from the Knight's Way into the depths of the forest.

The walk we have selected follows a circular route, taking in the remains of a 12th century

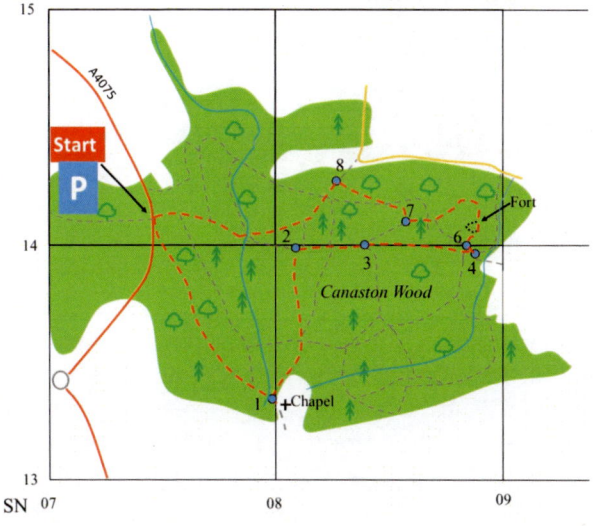

chapel and an Iron Age fort. The going is mainly smooth, not too hilly, but it can get muddy underfoot after rain

The walk begins (and ends) at the car park (SN 0745 1415) on the eastern side of the A4075. As you leave the car park, the Knight's Way leads off to the left, through a wide metal gate. An information sign put here by Natural Resources Wales tells of plans to convert these woods from pine trees to broadleaf over the next 100 years. We will return to the Knight's Way later on this walk but for now, our route lies along another path, the one that is in front of you as you come out of the car park and which sets off parallel to the main road but soon bends off to the left away from the sound of traffic. The path has the feel of a drover's track, with banks either side.

This part of the walk is well-covered by trees which will keep out heavy showers and strong sun. Initially, the pattern seems to be for tall pines in the background and deciduous trees close to the path. The mixture of tall pines and deciduous trees seems a good compromise between our need for timber and providing interest for walkers on the path. Soon the deciduous trees thin out and the woods are mostly pines, but they are spaced enough to allow light for greenery – mainly ferns – on the ground.

The path emerges into a clearing with the broad bowl of a valley to the left. Behind you there are fine views over the tops of the trees to the village of Robeston Wathen and beyond. On a clear day you can see the Preseli Hills. Pass the turning to the left at **1** (SN 0800 1333) and follow the stony path to a gate on your left. In the field, through this gate, you can see the ruins of Mounton Chapel. According to the Royal Commission on Ancient and Historical Monuments in Wales, worship has probably taken place on this site since the 12th or 13th century. The building was renovated in 1743 and was in use until 1948. Many a pilgrim would have stopped here on their way to St David's and knights could have called here at the start or end of a Crusade. The chapel is a sad sight now, though, surrounded by an impenetrable ring of bushes and brambles with only the roof visible over the top. It reminded us a little of the castle in the Sleeping Beauty around which a thorny hedge grows while the Princess sleeps. A gallant knight is certainly needed here to hack his way through the hedge and wake this chapel with a kiss.

Return down the stony path to junction 1 and turn right. We passed an old waymark placed here by Dyfed County Council, the administrative authority from 1974 until 1996 when Pembrokeshire was reinstated as the county. This is a delightful path, mostly straight with pines on the left and broadleaf trees to the right. You pass through a clearing, walk under some tall oaks and then join a wide path at **2** (SN 0813 1399). This is the Knight's Way. Turn right to continue with this walk.

The Knight's Way in this part is broad and stony underfoot; there is plenty of room for a knight and his charger to pass by. The way is open to horses and bicycles. We didn't see any horses on our visits, but there were cyclists and plenty of walkers. It is good to see the woodland here being so well used. The trees beside the path are broadleaf – beech, oak, ash and birch, with fir trees growing in the space behind. The pines are telegraph-pole straight and well-spaced; their tops swaying slightly in a gentle breeze.

At **3** (SN 0844 1397), the path emerges into a clearing, with the main track appearing to curve away to the right. Our route, though - and the Knight's way - lies straight ahead, and almost due east. There are five paths merging at this clearing and, counting clockwise from the one you have arrived on, the one you want is number 3. The path narrows soon after you start on it and plunges into dense woodland. We met a lone walker here and said a polite hello. We got no reply, which was discouraging but very rare. Walkers usually like to share a few words about how they are enjoying themselves and what they have seen.

The path now takes you steadily downhill under good tree cover with banks either side. Shortly after a signposted path to the right, there is a path to the left (4, SN 0892 1390). A little way below you from this spot, you will see a ford across a small stream. On our visit there was a pattern of tiny stationary waves on the surface of this stream. This pattern appears in shallow water flowing fast over rough ground. As the flow speeds up and slows down over the little hills and hollows, the water surface takes on the same shape as the solid floor beneath the flow. The stationary waves match the shape of the stream bed and the water flows through the pattern of the waves which are locked in place above the matching pattern of the floor. We noticed that there was also a criss-crossing pattern of smaller waves, and these too were fixed in position. A hydrodynamicist could have a lot of fun interpreting this patch of moving water but for the rest of us it is just fascinating to watch these waves and wonder about the forces that make them.

To get to the remains of the iron-age fort, take the turning offered at junction 4, skirting round the wooden fence that covers half the path. Climb for a short way and turn left at 5, continuing under a dense low canopy of holly and beech trees. In a short while, turn right at **6** (SN 0886 1397) onto a path which takes you to the fort. There isn't much to see at first. As you reach the top of the incline, the path cuts through the fort embankment, which is visible to the left, although much covered in trees and undergrowth.

The Iron Age, which in Wales lasted from about 800BC until the arrival of the Romans, was a time of prolific building of hillforts. More than 600 are known about today. The one in Canaston Woods (if it is indeed an Iron Age fort: Cadw, the Welsh government's historic environment service, are not sure but think it is likely) is certainly not the best preserved. But it is still impressive. The earthworks, all made by hand, enclose a space about 80 metres across. The protective bank around this area has, on its outside, a flat-bottomed ditch, several metres wide. Potential invaders would have to cross the ditch and then climb the bank which is several metres high. The residents must have felt pretty safe inside this fort.

The far bank of the fort is also visible (at SN 0884 1414). On a whim, we left the footpath here and ventured into the woods, ducking under branches and stepping over un-evenness in the ground to climb the bank. The earthworks are still very clear after more than two thousand years, and you can see the top of the bank stretching off to the south-west into the woods. From inside the fort, there is a gentle climb up to the top of the bank and then there is a sharp drop down to the wide ditch below. Armed

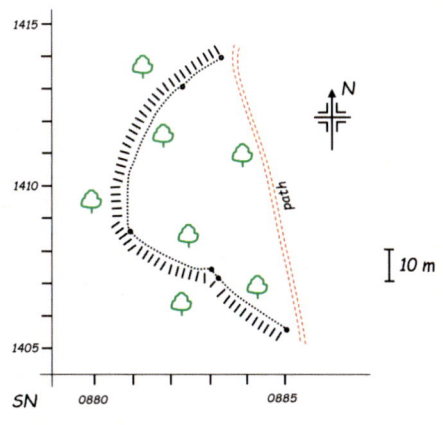

with a sharp iron axe or sword, you could deal severe blows to tired invaders climbing towards you. We edged our way along the top of the bank, shimmying around trees and taking the occasional GPS reading. A complete anti-clockwise loop of the bank, back to the path didn't take too long and we were able to draw the rough sketch map you see here.

Returning to the path and walking northwards, your way curves around to the left. The nature of the woodland is different here. The path is narrow and feels more off the beaten track. There are tall pines to your left and deciduous trees – mostly beech – on your right. At **7** (SN 0861 1416), we turned right where the path runs downhill to a fork, where we again turned right. Keeping right takes you around the outer edge of the woods; turning left at any point will take you back to the clearing and the Knight's Way. The path gets very narrow here with branches close overhead. Any knight who chose this route would have to breathe in (and take his suit of armour off) to get through. There are plenty of oak, beech, holly and birch trees, small and large, and tall pines off to the left.

The path emerges onto a newly-laid and newly-fenced part at **8** (SN 0829 1429). It is so smart that we had the feeling that we had inadvertently stepped into private property. The signs soon reassured us though that this is a public path. We took the second path on the left, which is smooth. It would be possible for a wheelchair to pass along here. There is a

gentle climb to a fork, where we kept to the right and then you pass through two sets of fencing in the curious shape of a cross. It is difficult to imagine what these bits of fence are for. The path now leads downhill, where you cross a stream by a wooden bridge, then there is a gentle climb to re-join the Knight's Way where you turn right to return to the Car Park.

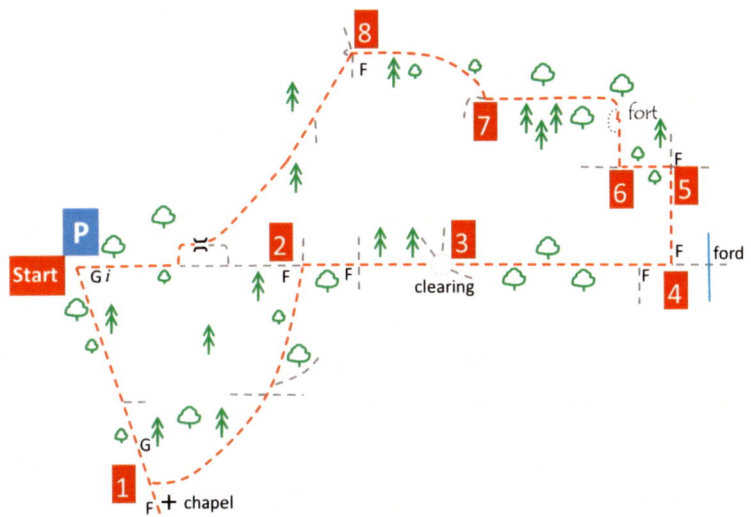

Rowan

Rowan, or mountain ash, are hardy trees, often found growing alone on a mountain side where no other tree can survive. They are also colourful and are a favourite in gardens, not least because their bright red berries attract birds. Their feathery leaves are paired on the branch in groups of up to eight, with an extra leaf pointing the way at the end, in the manner of ash trees. In spring, the Rowan has lovely white blossom and the scarlet berries in the autumn are a real eye-catcher.

Walk 12	**Minwear Forest**

A 7km circular walk through mixed forest. Mostly level along a good path. Allow 2.5 hours.

Minwear is a mixture of broadleaf trees and evergreens, with a history of providing wood for local industries, including shipbuilding and the ironworks at the site now occupied by Blackpool Mill. Natural Resources Wales provide an information board at the car park and suggest a one-hour circular walk. We chose a longer route which takes in the full length of the  wood as it runs along the Eastern Cleddau River and on which you will see the Sisters' House, whose purpose is an intriguing mystery, and a church operated at one time by the Knights of St. John. The walk is easy, mostly level, with occasional dips into a valley to cross a stream by a wooden bridge or boardwalk. Part of the walk takes you out of the forest, along the edge of an open field, and there is a pleasant straight stretch, mostly under trees, along a bridleway.

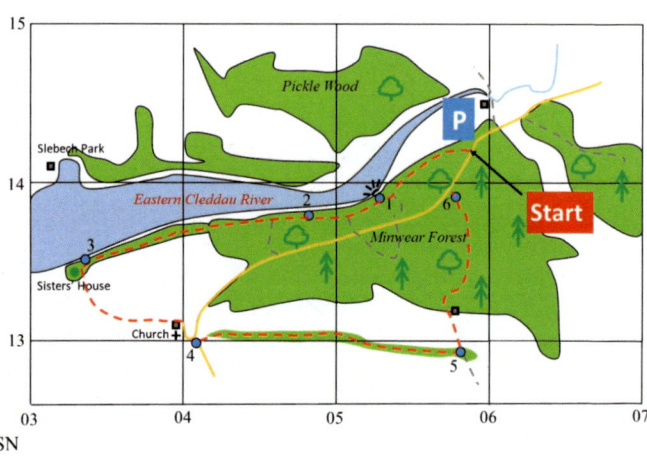

88

The first part of the walk is part of the Landsker Borderlands Trail, a long-distance path following the line between the traditionally Welsh-speaking north of Pembrokeshire and the English-speaking south (sometimes called 'Little England beyond Wales'). Landsker is a Norse word for borderland.

The car park, complete with a few potholes but with plenty of room, is located at OS grid point SN 0585 1426, on the minor road that passes Blackpool Mill. Begin the walk by heading west out of the car park, through the green metal gate. You are immediately plunged into dense woodland (birch and sycamore) as you follow a very broad path. It is noticeable that this path (and this is probably a general rule) is wide near the parking area but gets steadily narrower as you travel into the woods. Cross a bridge over a stream bed and take the gentle climb up the other side of the valley past the path leading off to the left.

At **1** there is a narrow path on the right leading down to a bench and a lookout point over the Eastern Cleddau River. In the distance, to the west and on the far bank, you can see the buildings of Slebech Hall, now a hotel.

Re-joining the main path and heading west, you arrive at a picnic area with carved benches. There is then a bit of a scramble down to some wooden bridges, after which you climb up steps to the path crossing at **2** (SN 0476 1380). If you turn right at this junction you can get down to the river bank. The river here is tidal – the mud banks are a good indicator of that – and the space you have here and the saltiness of the water in front of you will change with the tide.

Climbing back up to the main path and continuing westward, you take a detour around a field which comes between you and the river. The path then dips down into a valley and up some steps with a boardwalk across the stream at the bottom of the valley. At **3** (SN 0330 1359), the path turns left following the fence on the right-hand side. There is a footpath marked on the OS map leading

down to the river here. It is possible to scramble down through the trees but the path is not clear and there are no views when you do get to the bottom. Close to the river bank we spotted the characteristic knobbly green fruits of an Alder tree. Following the main path round to the left you will see some ruins to the right beyond the fence. These are the remains of the property marked on the OS map as the Sisters' House. The buildings are now covered in greenery and difficult to see but they are certainly old, referred to in a document of 1546. Their exact age and purpose are unknown. The name brings to mind a convent; from the sixth century onwards, pilgrims would travel through this area on their way to the cathedral at St David's. The Sisters' House may have offered a resting place and support for pilgrims, but we really don't know. It is also possible that it was built for more secular purposes, as farm buildings operated by the Slebech Estate which owned the land here in the 16th century.

Continue on the path to emerge from the woods through a kissing gate and walk along the edge of arable fields to Minwear Farm. The OS map has the path passing the farmhouse to the left but that way seems blocked today. Pass the farmhouse on your right instead and you emerge onto a small country lane with the church of St Womar on your right. It is worth pausing a while here to look at this church. According to the Dyfed Archaelogical Trust, the construction of the nave probably dates back to the 13th century. The church was the property of the Knights Hospitaller of St John, who helped crusaders and pilgrims travel to the Holy Land and had a base at Slebech. Look out for the stained-glass window showing the 8-pointed Maltese Cross, which became a symbol of the Knights of St John. The building is now owned by the Church in Wales.

Carrying on along the lane, you come to a T-junction. On your right here you will see a bridleway sign leading off to the left at **4**. Take this bridleway, which is a pleasant walk, initially with banks on either side and later with plenty of tree cover. Arable fields lie either side of this bridleway and at their corners you cross farm tracks connecting the fields on either side. This is not strictly a woodland walk but there is plenty to look for in the hedgerows. The path has an ancient feel to it and we wondered if this was a track used by the pilgrims on their way to and from St. David's.

At the end of the bridleway, at **5** (SN 0582 1292), you reach a lane. From here you can see the rides at Oakwood Park over the tops of the trees and occasionally hear the screams. Turn left, pass the lodge and enter Minwear Forest for the last leg of the walk. The trees are very tall here, both evergreen and deciduous. When the wind blows strongly enough the tops sway back and forth and rustle in the breeze. It is fascinating to stand, looking up, watching this movement. It seemed to us that the pitch of the sound from the pine trees was slightly different to that from the broadleaf trees, but it was difficult to be sure. This ancient sound of the trees is certainly much kinder to the ear and brain than that coming from the Oakwood rides. Continue along the broad, hard track, pass the log piles on your left and plantations on your right. The path now runs downhill past some brightly coloured houses to join the road at **6** (0574 1393). Turn right here and follow the road back to the car park.

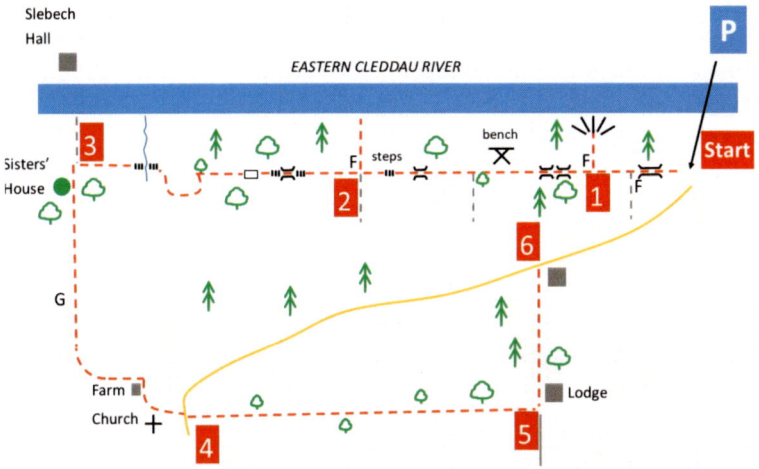

The Swaying of Trees

The force of the wind on a tree pushes it sideways, mainly near the top where the trunk is thinner and more flexible. The pressure applied by the wind is balanced by the springiness of the trunk. When the wind stops, or slackens, the forces are no longer in balance. The tree rights itself, overshoots the vertical and then sways backwards and forwards in the simple harmonic motion of a pendulum or a weight on a spring. The period of the oscillation – the time for one full back and forth swing – depends on the mass of the tree and the springiness of the trunk. For the tall trees we were watching in Minwear forest, the period was about 5 seconds.

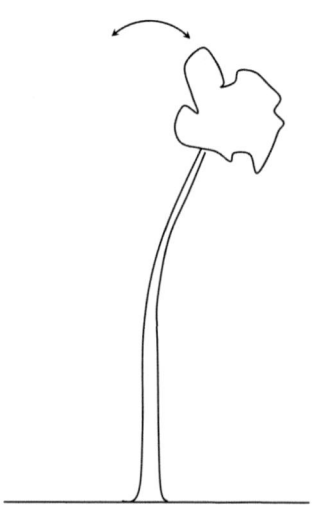

As the tree sways, the trunk may creak a little as the wood is squeezed and stretched. It is important to the tree to be able to flex in this way. The swaying at the tip of the tree prevents the movement being passed to the roots. In a forest, the most flexible trees are found round the edge, where they can protect the inner trees from the full force of the wind.

Something similar happens when the wind blows over a leaf but now the small mass and greater flexibility of the leaf stem create a higher frequency oscillation. The leaves shake in the wind, creating a sound which is audible to our ear. The leaves *rustle*. Pine needles are less flexible, but the wind blowing over them creates a wake of tiny vortices. The rapid variations in pressure make a different sound to the shaking of broadleaf leaves. It is quite possible that the different trees in Minwear forest were creating sounds of different pitch.

The sound of trees is therapeutic. It is rooted deep in our psyche, planted there when our ancestors huddled together in forests at night, listening to the reassuring song of the trees as they drifted off to sleep.

Alder

Alder is native to the United Kingdom and is often found close to water, where it thrives. It is most easily identified by its flowers, or catkins. Both male and female catkins form on the same tree. The male ones are longer and thinner and  the female green and knobbly, on stalks. The leaves are oval-shaped, almost round and flat, or even slightly indented, at the end.

Alder has a symbiotic relationship with a nitrogen-fixing bacterium which turns nitrogen from the air into fertilizer for the tree. In consequence, Alder can grow in poor soil, short of nitrate, and it is amongst the first trees to colonise former industrial land.

Alder wood is tough when wet and resists rotting. It was traditionally used for boat-building and for structures which needed to stay strong underwater. The green female catkins can be used to dye items of clothing an attractive caramel colour.

Walk 13　Little Milford

A short walk, just 3km, but with some steep sections. Allow an hour and a half.

Little Milford is small wood set on a hillside running down to the Western Cleddau estuary. There are fine walks to be had here, historical interest in the coal workings and interesting estuary views. It is, though, easy to become  disorientated on the network of paths which twist and turn upon themselves, so take your wits with you, or a compass. The land here is now owned and managed by the National Trust and, according to their website, this woodland goes back to at least the

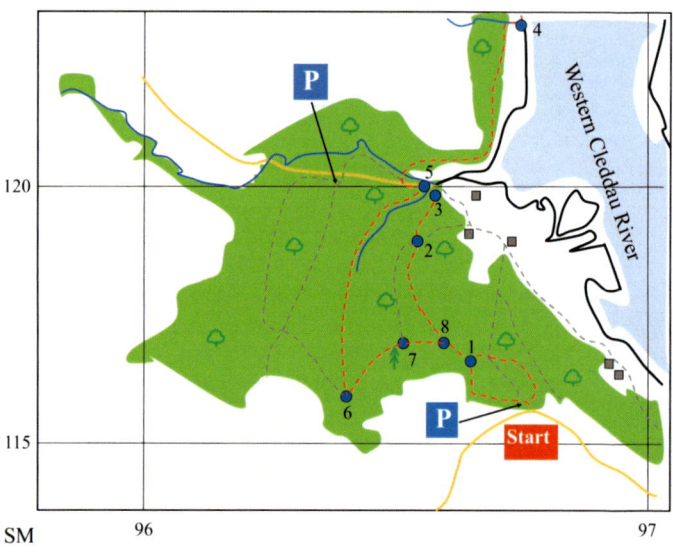

11th century. In the early days, trees were used locally for fuel and building and then, probably about 600 years ago, coal was discovered underground. The coal mined here and at the other mines around the neighbouring village of Hook was a particularly good anthracite which burned hot without making a lot of smoke. It is said that Queen Victoria requested Hook anthracite for use on the Royal Yacht because it didn't leave sooty marks on the Royal personages walking on deck. The last pit here closed in 1959 and the estate turned to cultivating commercial timber. In 1975, the land was donated to the National Trust who have carried out a programme of harvesting the conifer trees and planting native species in their place.

The walk starts at the car park (SM 9677 1161) on the road between the villages of Freystrop and Hook. The 308 bus from Haverfordwest to Burton will take you to Hook and you can walk back to the car park, or the driver will probably drop you off right at the start of the walk if you ask. There are three paths leading from the car park, two by the information board at the western end, but we took the third path which leaves from the other end of the car park, through the gate with the National Trust sign. You soon come to an information board and a winch, restored by volunteers, from the old coal mine. At the time of our visit, the winch was wrapped in red and white tape which spoiled its looks, but interesting detail was visible, including the ratchet which stopped the winch unwinding when the operator paused for a rest and the maker's name, Stephens of Pembroke.

There is a bench here where you can have a picnic, but the view of the estuary, which looks as though it could be a very fine one, was obscured by the trees. Continue the walk by taking the path leading downhill, passing the winch on your right. The National Trust's scheme of planting native trees can be seen to be working here. There is a good variety of young trees, including oak, beech and holly, and they are thriving. Carry straight on at the point where another path crosses, with steps to the left and a steep descent to the right. According to M.R. Connop-Price's account of Pembrokeshire's coal fields, the gradient on your right here is the

former site of a tramway from the colliery to the quay on the river. The incline is 400 yards long and coal trucks were pulled up by rope (possibly using the winch that you passed earlier). Soon, you arrive at the junction **1** (SM 9666 1169), where you bear right. Follow this slightly gravelly path downhill, past oak and sycamore and, in autumn, some pink-leaved guilder roses, which stand out amidst the greenery. According to the Woodland Trust, guilder roses are an indication of an ancient woodland, that is one that has been around since the year 1600 in Wales. The bright red berries are an important food for birds.

The gravel gives way to bare rock, shaped roughly in steps which take you downhill. You could follow this route to the bottom, where you would turn left, but it is more pleasant to take the shortcut at **2** (SM 9659 1187). Here there are two paths leading off to the left. Take the second of these into the trees and, surprisingly, there is a small children's playground. We didn't think this looked like an official playground, just one someone has made for little ones to enjoy. It is a

great spot to take young children. The walk continues straight ahead and downhill from here, passing the playground on your right and following a mulchy path under tall trees. You emerge through an opening in the fence at **3** (SM 9663 1196). In front of you is a lane, leading to left and right and, beyond that a stream with muddy banks.

It is possible to cross the brook, called the Red Water, here, but it would be a messy job. The stream can be wide and there is plenty of gloopy mud to negotiate. Someone, however, has hand-written on the finger post 'footbridge, 50 yards' and sure enough, a short way upstream (turning left onto the lane) there is a perfectly fine wooden footbridge which will get you to the other side of this stream as clean as when you started. It is heart-warming to come across helpful information like this. Someone has taken the trouble to let other walkers know there is a better way; there is no other explanation for that sign. We sometimes tend to believe these days that unselfish helpfulness is on the way out, that people are only out to help themselves, but that's clearly not the case here. Nor is it just our generation that thinks that the world is becoming selfish.

In J.B. Priestley's novel *The Good Companions*, published in 1929, there is a short speech: 'There isn't too much good companionship left, is there? People don't pull together so much. A lot of people are out for a good time – but it's nearly always their own good time and nobody else's'. Well, walkers make good companions. Even those you have never met but who leave helpful signs.

Cross the wooden bridge and follow the path around to the right, heading towards the river. You pass through a small gate and down some steps and then ignore the turning to the left to arrive at the banks of the river with interesting views in both directions (there are some stepping stones here; they seemed a little redundant on our visit, but probably this place is muddy when wet). The river is tidal here and the views will change a great deal with the state of the tide. We arrived at low tide and the wide estuary had just a little stream winding its way down the centre, through much larger expanses of grey mud. Where can all this mud come from and why does it settle here? One idea is that the mud is brought, in very low concentrations, by the river, eroded from land upstream. When the clay particles encounter salt water in the estuary for the first time, the change in the chemistry causes them to stick together in clumps. The greater weight of the clumps makes them settle out into the mud banks. It is, however, difficult to reconcile these processes happening on a microscopic scale with the great swathes of mud you see here. Perhaps something else entirely different has happened: the mud has arrived from the other direction, brought from the sea by the tide and deposited as the flow slackens at high water. Great mud banks like this are certainly a characteristic of tidal waters everywhere.

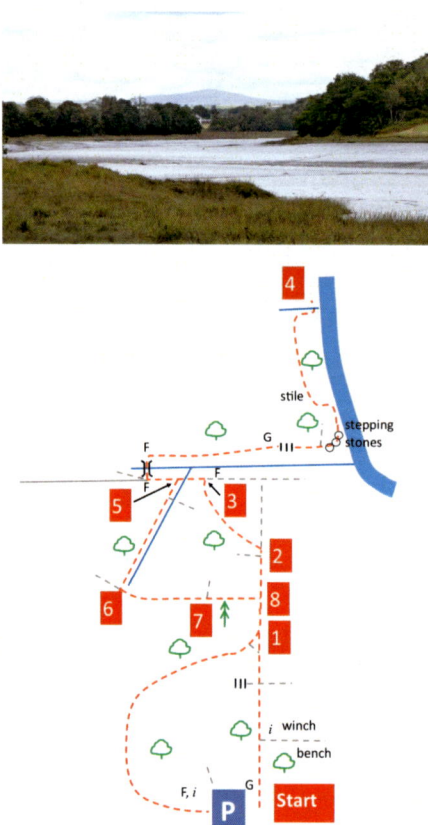

The path continues along the river bank, under trees on the landward side bringing you to a stile which you cross, climb up a bank and then follow the path that runs along the edge of the wood. There is a drop down to the river bank on your right and a slope up through the trees on your left. This is a fine bit of walking, different to the rest of this walk and, in truth, we have left Little Milford woods here, certainly the National Trust part of them. It would be possible to follow this path along the side of the river for some way (the OS map suggests you could walk along the river bank to Haverfordwest from here). But we decided that we had gone beyond the title of this walk and so turned around at the point **4** (SM 9676 1236) where the path drops down to the river bank once again and there are views upriver to the Preseli Hills in the extreme distance.

Retrace your steps back to the wooden footbridge across the stream. You could return from here to the car park the way you came but, for variety, we chose the path which leaves the lane at a point (**5**, SM 9661 1195) just to the west of a stream. Follow this broad path, grassy underfoot, past the wooden plank bridge on your left and up the hill with the stream on your left-hand side. At the T-junction (**6** SM 9640 1162), turn left. Keep right at **7** (SM 9645 1165), walking past some pines until you arrive back at the path you followed initially down to the river (**8** SM 9659 1174). Turn right here, keep right at junction **1** and walk up the hill back to the car park.

Ash

Ash trees can be identified by their leaves formed in pairs on either side of thin branches like the wings of aeroplanes lined up on the runway. At the end of the branch is a single leaf, pointing the way for the planes to take off. The leaves can move to follow the sun and can form a dense, shady canopy.

Ash trees are native to the UK and common in Pembrokeshire. The wood is hard and can withstand knocks and shocks. It is an excellent material for making tool handles: for axes and hammers, for example. It was (and still

is) the wood of choice for the oars used in the boats of the Royal Navy. The frames (but not the chassis) of Morgan sports cars are made from Ash specially grown for the purpose.

European Ash trees are currently struggling with a disease called Ash dieback. This is a fungus, originating in Asia and against which our native trees have no natural defence. It appears as dark patches on the leaves in summer and will kill the tree. Tragically, we are likely to lose most of these beautiful and useful trees.

How does water get to the top of a tree?

This may seem like a non-question. Why shouldn't it? Water evaporates from the leaves and is replaced by water that is sucked up from the ground. The trouble with this simple answer is that there is a limit to how high you can suck water that is being pulled down by earth's gravity.

Imagine that you dip one end of a long hose pipe into a bucket of water and carry the other end up to the top of a tree. You attach a pump to the top of the pipe and suck the water up the pipe. If your pump is a very good one which creates a perfect vacuum at the top of the pipe, you will find that the highest you can suck the water up is about 32 feet or 10 metres. The water will

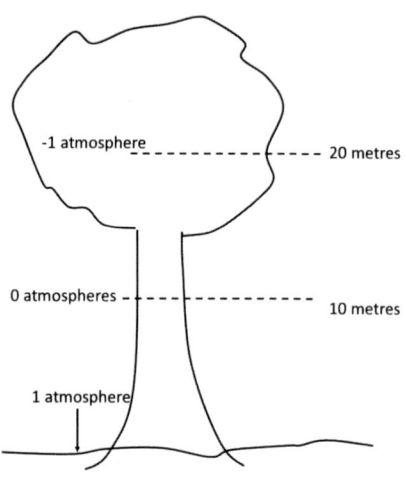

climb no higher, no matter how hard you suck. The pressure at the bottom of the pipe is one atmosphere, or 15 pounds per square inch. The pressure at the top of the pipe is zero atmospheres. The *difference* in pressure – one atmosphere – is just able to balance the weight of water in the pipe. This is the principle of the mercury barometer. Mercury is a lot heavier than water and atmospheric pressure is able to support a column of mercury about 30 inches high. As atmospheric pressure changes, the top of the column moves a little up and down the barometer.

Lots of trees, even in Pembrokeshire, are taller than 10 metres. How do they manage to get water right to the top of the tree? The trick they use is to create a *negative* pressure in the tubes (called xylem) rising up through the trunk and branches. The water pressure in the xylem falls from one atmosphere at the ground, to zero atmospheres at a height of 10 metres and then it becomes negative. At a height of 20 metres, the water pressure is *minus* one atmosphere. The pressure difference from top to bottom is now two atmospheres and that can hold up a water column of 20 metres.

Negative pressure is a strange concept. In water under positive pressure, the molecules are squeezed together. In water under negative pressure, they are pulled apart, stopped from being torn asunder by the attractive forces between water molecules. It is this ability of water to withstand negative pressure that allows trees to grow to great heights. Gasses do not have the ability to withstand negative pressure and so it is important for the tree to keep the xylem full of water with no air pockets.

At the top of the tree, the water is transferred to the leaves. The leaves have tiny pores, called stomata, on their surface, and here the water comes into contact with the outside world. The pressure in the air outside the leaf is one atmosphere and the pressure in the water in the stomata is less than one atmosphere (if the tree is taller than 10 metres the pressure will be negative). The difference in pressure produces a force pushing the water out of the leaf and back down the xylem the way it came. Trees have found a clever way to stop this happening. Pressure is a force acting on an area - pounds per square inch, for example. The cross-sectional area of each stoma is tiny and the force produced by the pressure difference is also tiny. It can be resisted by the small forces of attraction between the water molecules and the walls of the stomata. Each stoma puts a small holding force on the water within it. The accumulation of forces from millions of stomata keeps the water column clipped in place at the top like the pegs which hold up the washing or the belt on your trousers.

Trees have mastered the forces of nature to enable them to grow to great heights. There are limits to how much negative pressure water can resist, though, which is thought to be about 13 or 14 atmospheres. This would place an absolute limit on the height of trees of about 150 metres. The tallest trees in the world, the giant redwoods of California, get close to this height.

Walk 14 Lawrenny Wood

A 5km circular walk with some steep sections. Allow 2 hours.

This is a charming circular walk which packs a surprising amount of variety into its short length. There are gentle sections on country lanes, a passage through an ancient oak forest and a walk on the edge of the mudflats of a tidal river. For most of the walk,  you are accompanied by views of the Daugleddau river through the trees. You will see a Norman Church, an ancient castle and the birthplace of one of our most successful thriller writers. Much of the path is on good tracks and lanes but there are places where it gets a bit narrow and crumbly. The walk along the top of the tide mark could get wet. So, boots are essential and care is also needed, but you would have to work hard to get lost on this one.

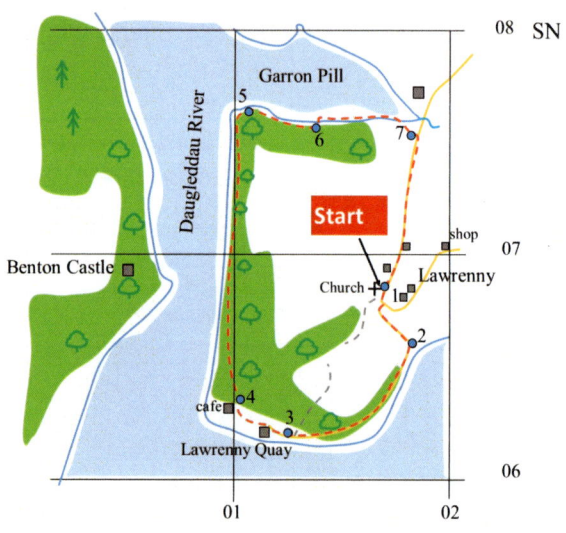

There are a number of convenient starting points for this walk. We chose the pretty village of Lawrenny where there are a few places to park a car tidily, including by the village church of St Caradoc (**1** SN 01696 06933). It is worth taking some time at the beginning or end of the walk to look at this old place of worship and its grounds. Like many rural churches in the area, it has parts dating back to the 12th century. It is also a good place for tree-spotting. There is a large lime tree by the gateway and some great yews with multi-columned trunks standing in the churchyard.

Set off on the road heading downhill from the church and turn right along the lane signposted Lawrenny Quay. Look out for the strata in the rocks supporting the wall on your right. The foundations of the wall are layers of bedrock lying at an angle to the horizontal. On your left (at **2**, SN 0185 0671) there is what looks like a tumbled down gatepost with the inscription 'erected 1918'. We decided, however, that a gatepost would more likely carry the name of the house behind the gates rather than the year of construction. Could it be a war memorial? But then why had it been allowed to fall into ruin? The members of the Hook Historical Society provided an answer. The gateposts were erected by the Lawrenny estate (it was common to put dates on constructions at the time), but later knocked down to allow something large, possibly a boat, to be towed to the quay.

There are certainly marks of history around here. Lawrenny may be off the beaten track on the road network but it was and is an important hub on the waterway. The Daugleddau, Creswell and Carew rivers converge on Lawrenny Quay and this junction would have been well known to the crews of the small boats carrying coal and limestone and other goods over the centuries. Boats were built at the quay and there was a ferry service operated from here in living memory. In the 1940's this was a base for flying boats – Supermarine Walrus and Catalinas – used for reconnaissance missions to support the convoys crossing the Atlantic.

Pass the pub, the Lawrenny Arms, and go through the gate posts at **3** (SN 0130 0622) towards the boats you can see ahead. Follow the path around past the buildings on your left and the campsite on the right. There is a café here, and then a boatyard where children must be accompanied by adults. Straight after the boatyard you are into the woods (at **4**, SN 0104 0628). Here we met a fellow walker who asked if we were going upstream. We said we were, although we hadn't thought of it in those terms.

Follow the path as it curves behind the caravans on the right. The signs here tell you that this is a permissive path rather than a right of way. Soon, though, you enter the part of the woods owned by the National Trust. The path narrows here and there are tree roots to look out for. The branches of the ancient oak trees all around you twist in magical ways. The route takes you gently uphill along the side of a hill sloping up to your right and down to the Daugleddau river on your left.

After a while, the very white Benton Castle comes into view across the river. This is an old building, probably built about 800 years ago, originally as a fortification. It fell into ruin but was restored in the 20th century and is now a private home. In the 1890's Henry Thornhill Timmins visited the ruin and wrote: *Little remains of the fabric save the principal tower, the base of which is circular in form, the upper works being corbelled out and fashioned into an octagon* (the octagon seems to have been lost in the restoration). *With the arched gateway, flanked by a portion of a second drum-tower, these crumbling ruins form a picturesque group, whose features are almost lost amidst the luxuriant foliage that runs riot over all.*

Don't be too distracted by this eye-catcher, you need to watch your step along here, the path is eroding on the downside and the slope to the river is quite steep.

Something else caught our eye. We had arrived at a time when the tide was on the flood and there was a feint but discernible foam line visible on the surface, running parallel to the shore and a little closer to our side than the other. This foam line was to stay with us for the next mile or so. It was a line of cream-coloured material floating on the surface and curling up on itself in places. The line marked a difference in the roughness of the water. The waves, though not large, were definitely bigger on the far side of the line than our side. Foam lines like this are usually caused by a convergence of currents. Surface water travels towards the line from both sides. When the water reaches the foam line it sinks, leaving any floating material: twigs, leaves, oils and scum, on the surface.

The path continues narrowly, sometimes with a scramble up some steps cut in the rock face and sometimes stepping over a stream in a dip. Hands are occasionally needed here as well as feet. The main river now begins to bend away towards the left and there are fine views upstream obscured to some extent by the trees. The path then takes a sharp turn to the right and enters a clearing (**5** SN 0108 0767) where there is a wooden hut with a notice telling us that it was 'refurbished by Castle School in 2018'. This would be a fine spot for watching foam lines but it is probably intended to be a bird hide. Sadly, it is not very congenial. There was litter inside at the time of our visit and part of the floor had given way. There are fine views from here, though, over a tributary of the Daugleddau called Garron Pill. A group of buildings clustered together on the far side of the Pill on a hill above the east bank of the Daugleddau looks like it could be a small village but is actually a farm, Coedcanlas, the birth-place of author and national hunt jockey Dick Francis.

The path now follows the south bank of Garron Pill. A 'Pill' in this sense is a stretch of tidal waterway. Although the word crops up in various parts of the country, it is most common in those counties of south Wales and south-west England that lie either side of the Bristol Channel and Severn estuary. We watched a

group of swans travelling upstream, taking a free ride on the flooding tide. Steps at **6** (SN 0140 0761) take you down to the shore and you head inland (to the right) along the high-tide mark. Here there is a small clay cliff with trees dangling over it on your right and mudflats with winding channels on your left. There are sounds of water birds calling and waders leave their footprints in the mud. It really is a special world, quite different from what has gone before on this walk. This is one of those special places where the boundary between the land and the sea becomes blurred. The road that crosses the top of the Pill can be covered by salt water (there is a raised foot bridge for pedestrians) and the greenery is able to withstand regular dunking in brine. The path takes you back on to proper land again at the top of the Pill (7, SN 0175 0762). Follow the metal fence on your right across the open space until you join a lane. Turn right here and follow the lane back to Lawrenny church.

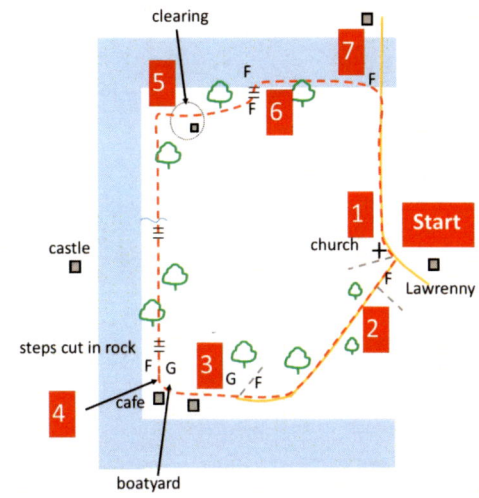

After this walk, we visited the café on Lawrenny Quay, which served us well. You can get ice creams on a hot day and tea and sandwiches on a cold one. There is a changing menu of hot meals. The café uses local produce, aims to reduce waste and eliminate single-use plastic. It caters for vegans and has gluten-free options. There are seats inside and out and, wherever you sit, you can gaze out onto the estuary where flying boats once carved their way through the water.

Lime

Limes are another of those trees that have oval, pointed leaves with serrated edges. One thing that might help you to distinguish this tree from others with similar leaves is that the leaf is lobed, or heart-

shaped, where it joins the stem. Another distinguishing feature is the little round fruits on long stalks. A good place to look for limes is in ornamental parks and gardens.

Walk 15 Amroth

A walk of about 7 km from the sea up one river valley and down another. Allow 2 ½ hours.

Amroth lies in the south-east corner of the county at one end of the Pembrokeshire Coast Path. The sight of the sparkling sea as you come down the hill into the village is great for lifting the spirits. The information board in the car park explains that the village grew in the nineteenth  century when coal and iron ore were mined in the area. The beach was used to practice the D-Day landings. The walk we have chosen is Y-shaped. You set off from the coast up the leg of the Y to Colby Woodland Gardens, owned by the National Trust. There are then the two arms of the Y, each a woodland walk along a tumbling stream. You can either go up and down each arm, coming back to the centre, or take a short cut across the top of the Y.

A public car park is available in Amroth (take the turning signposted to St

108

Elidyr's church). There is a charge during the summer and donations are invited out of season. The 351 bus service running from Tenby to Pendine stops close by. Public toilets are available not far away, on the western end of the sea front. There are plenty of benches on the promenade where you can put on walking boots and admire the view.

The walk starts along the 'Knight's Way' marked on OS maps. Head up the lane signposted towards St Elidyr's church and after two hundred metres or so look out for the footpath leading off to the left at **1** (SN 1623 0715). It is easy to miss this turning because it looks as if it could be a private entrance to a house. The lane bends away to the right here and our path bears to the left, past a fingerpost pointing to Colby. After passing a couple of houses you enter woodland on a broad stony path with the river down below. The river is no more than a stream, really, and we couldn't find a name for it. Keep on this broad path, ignoring turnings to right and left. It is a half-mile walk to Colby Woodland gardens and this path is popular with dog walkers.

Colby gardens were mostly created in the early twentieth century and ownership was transferred to the National Trust in 1979. The site makes a pleasant stopping place on this walk. There are toilets and a café, benches for a picnic and you can practice your tree-identifying skills. Note that there is an entrance fee to the gardens for non-members of the National Trust, although you can pass through on the path for free and the café is open to everyone.

From Colby gardens go onto the lane which crosses the northern entrance and turn left along this lane. Walk past the first two signposted footpaths leading off to the right and then take the third exit at **2** (SN 1554 0819). When you turn right here you are faced with two options. One is a drive which curls around to the right and leads to some NT cottages. The one you want is the path which forks off to the left heading towards the stream. There is a

sign for the Knight's Way, or the Ffordd y Marchogion, here. This was the first we had noticed although we saw some others later on this walk. The Knight's Way crops up in other parts of this book but it is difficult to find information about it. Anyway, you are on it here!

The best part of this walk now begins. Up to this point we had not been experiencing the magic calming effect of woodland walks, but it soon kicked in once we left the lane behind and walked along this mulchy path under trees. It seems to us that the essential ingredients for a good woodland walk are trees overhead (and to the sides as far as the eye can see) and soft ground beneath your feet. A stream and spring flowers in bloom are a bonus. The path here fits the bill: your footsteps are accompanied by the sounds of a tumbling water and songbirds. The path climbs gently into the oak trees. Birds dozing in the early spring sunshine were startled by our approach and flew off in a flutter. At **3** (SN 1542 0889) the path leaves the stream and climbs diagonally up the side of the valley. The Knight's Way continues through the gate up to the junction at **4** (SN 1563 0939) where it bears left and crosses the A477. Our way at this junction, though, is to the right, following the path that leads southwards along the top edge of the woods. Oak trees fill the slope to your right. It was here that a large bird flew overhead, casting a shadow on the ground. Its beating wings made a similar sound to a panting dog and, at first, we thought it was a dog running up to us until we saw the shadow.

At **5** (SN 1560 0893) go through the gate on your left into an open field. The path here connects you to Pendeilo wood, which makes the other arm of the Y on this walk. Follow the path across the open fields, going through two gates. At one point, a short distance on your left, you can see the OS trig point, which is 137 metres above sea level.

Follow the path until it enters the woods through a gate at **6** (SN 1593 0892) and continue on the path along the top of the woods here. There are fine views across the wooded valley to your left. When you come to the gate at **7** (SN 1616 0886), turn left and take the path that winds its way down to the stream at **8** (SN 1626 0907). Violet flowers lined the sides of the path here and yellow gorse and white blackthorn blossom filled the hedgerows – the colours of nature in early spring. When you get to the junction at **8**, turn right and follow the stream. The land on your left soon becomes marshy – a great place for a dog to get muddy. This really is a magical place, with tangled oak trees growing in the shallow ponds at the bottom of the valley.

The path rises above the valley floor for a short while and then descends again by steps to the stream. Continue along this path, following the stream (and ignoring turnings to left and right) until you emerge back on the lane at Colby gardens at **9** (SN 1568 0814). Surprisingly, this path along the stream is not actually marked on our OS Explorer map of South Pembrokeshire, but it certainly exists and is well maintained. On one of our visits we met an employee of the National Trust who was replacing a signpost. He told us how much he loved this walk along the stream through Pendeilo woods, and quite rightly so. It is marvellous.

Return to Colby gardens and take the bridleway back down to the coast and Amroth.

After this walk, you might like to visit nearby Lanteague Wood. This may seem like a busman's holiday for woodland walkers but woods owned by the Woodland Trust are rare in Pembrokeshire. Lanteague Wood has a small car park at SN 17999 09539. The wood is composed mostly of young trees, seldom more than 20 feet tall growing close together and with the occasional footpath dividing up the blocks of planted trees. It is still possible to see, as you gaze in amongst the woods, how these native trees have been arranged in regular patterns: just like a conifer plantation but with deciduous trees instead. This is all just left here to be enjoyed and it will grow into a fine forest. How good is that? There is even a bench to sit on while you take off your boots.

The structure of trees

Leonardo Da Vinci, the great Renaissance artist and inventor, was interested in the structure of trees because he wanted them to look realistic in his drawings. His notebooks describe a rule he used to help him get trees looking right. The rule says, in essence, that at any height the sum of the cross-sectional area of all the branches is constant. The combined cross-sectional area of all the little twigs at the top of the tree is the same as the cross-sectional area of the trunk and also the same as the cross-sectional area of the branches half way up the tree. If your hands were strong enough, you could run them up the trunk of the tree, folding all the branches and twigs upwards and squeezing them together to remove any spaces and you would end up with a column of wood of constant diameter from top to bottom.

It's a remarkable observation, made 500 years ago by a genius, but it has to be admitted that it is unlikely that all trees will follow this rule exactly. Nature is powerful and trees will adapt their shape to make the most of local conditions. Nevertheless, a tree which has plenty of room to spread will follow something close to Leonardo's rule.

A tree that keeps the same cross section of wood as large branches divide into smaller branches has the interesting property that the branch patterns look the same on different scales. A branch the width of your arm that splits into smaller finger-width branches and then into twigs looks like a smaller version of the trunk dividing into big branches and then into smaller ones. The whole tree is made up of small-scale versions of itself. We automatically use this repetition of patterns from big to small scale when we sketch a natural looking tree. Mathematicians call this copying of patterns a *fractal* structure.

Trees have roots and a trunk to anchor them to the ground and support the weight of timber that sits on top. Branches grow from the trunk and then produce ever smaller branches to create a large canopy of leaves to catch the sunshine. A tree in which the cross-sectional area of the wood remains the same as you move through the range of branch sizes has no bottlenecks: water and nutrients can pass smoothly from the roots up to the leaves. This may be one reason trees follow Leonardo Da Vinci's rule. Computer simulations suggest that a tree which preserves the total cross-sectional area of wood in the different branch sizes is also particularly good at withstanding strong winds without being blown over. Naturally, trees have adopted a shape that makes them efficient and strong.

Walk 16 — Stackpole (northern section)

7.5 km, mostly circular and on woodland paths. Allow 2.5 hours.

The northern part of the Stackpole estate is owned, like the southern section (walk 17), by the National Trust. The woods here have no special scientific interest, however, and there isn't the fuss created by the lakes in the south. These woods provide a different experience to their more famous neighbour. This part of the estate is much quieter and the woods are thicker and more varied. The information board in the car park tells that the conifers lost in the storm of 2014 are being replaced by broadleaf trees including oak, hazel, wild cherry and sweet chestnut. The woods are criss-crossed by a variety of tracks and paths and there are a number of circuits that you could make out of them. The walk we have chosen takes in an old smokery, the handsome church at Stackpole Elidor, Stackpole Court and the shallow northern part of the lakes. There are plenty of places to stop and have a picnic. The going is typical of a woodland walk, there are some steep climbs and descents and the path can get very muddy in the rain, so boots are essential and a stick helpful. It is also easy to become disorientated on the twisting paths with few long views (especially in Castle Dock Wood) so a map and compass are a good idea.

While you are putting your boots on in the car park (SR 9799 9655), you can get any youngsters with you to look for the carved owl hidden not far away. That should keep them busy while you pay attention to your laces. Take a moment to read the information board and study the map. The tracks on the map (and on the finger

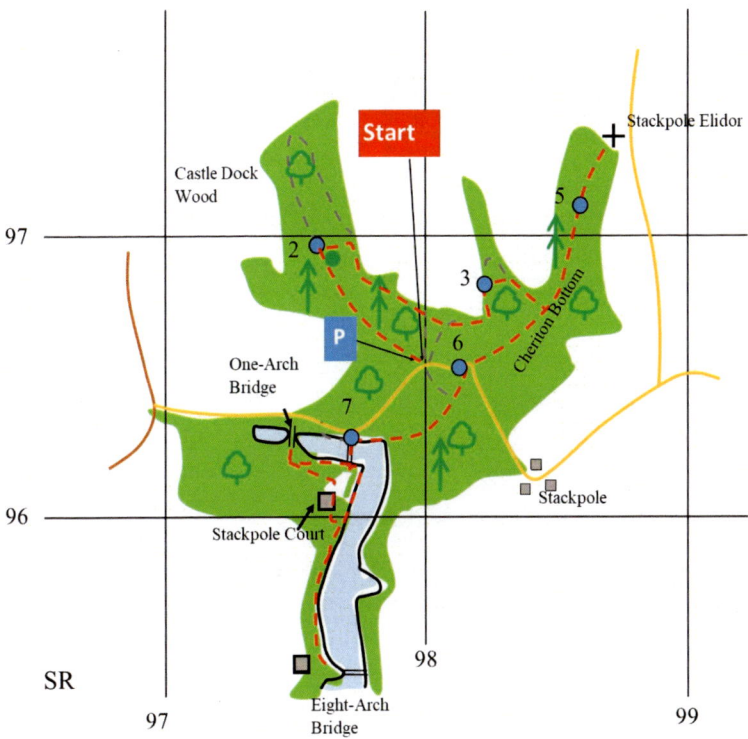

posts) are colour coded; it is the Castle Dock Woodland Adventure (3 miles, moderate) that we shall mostly be following. Set off northwards through the gate from the car park, following the broad track running slightly uphill. There is plenty of evidence here of the tall pines that once filled the forest, although now there are gaps between them in which newly planted broadleaf trees are growing up to the light. If you have arrived at the right time of year (November) you don't have to go far to find sweet chestnuts on the ground and the tree colours here will be beautiful.

Keep left at the clearing **1** (SR 9781 9682) and carry on up the broad path. Keep right where the path branches left over a stream and walk up the narrowing path to reach the Smoke House at **2** (9758 9695). There is a charming picnic table here, complete with mushroom-shaped stools. Smoke houses (also called smokeries) are buildings in which meat and fish are cured (or preserved) with smoke. We could find no information about this particular

smokery. Presumably it served the Stackpole estate although we can't understand why it should be so far from the main house (were these places so very smelly?). Anyway, it looks as though it has been many years since the building was used. Turn right here and follow the track round to the right and uphill towards the top edge of the woods. The path takes you among ferns and deciduous trees into a well-covered walk. Oak and Sycamore leaves lie underfoot and more leaves were falling in flurries from above as gusts of wind shook the trees. We could feel the stresses of daily life fading as the woods did their magic.

The path is joined by another coming from the north-west and it then takes you along the top edge of the woods with open fields visible through the trees to your left. There is a little chicane, or s-bend, where the path dips and rises again. Ignore the path leading off to your right, down the hill, and pass a picnic bench on your left. It can be slippy underfoot here, so be careful. There are a couple of paths down to the right which will take you back to the car park here if you need to pick up or drop off a coat. You now enter a beech plantation. On this autumn visit, the statuesque

beech trees stretched above us and the ground was crunchy with beech nuts. Very little can grow on the ground in a beech wood: beeches are not friendly to undergrowth. The signs here implore you to keep left,

sticking to the top of the slope. After a while, the path takes you back into mixed woodland, including sycamore and ash, and turns towards the north west. You are in a valley, running up towards Bangeston Hall. The aim here is to cross over to the other side of the valley as safely and pleasantly as possible. We took the signposted 'walking trail' turning at **3** (SR 9826 9682) which was a bit of a scramble down the slope and up the other side. If you want an easier

transit, carry on a little further up the valley and the path will then take you down some zig-zags and across a small wooden boardwalk. Either way, you can join the path on the far side of the valley, travelling south-east.

After a short while, this path will bring you to the junction **4** (9826 9684) where you turn first right and then left to join the broad track heading north-east into the delightfully named Cheriton Bottom. As you might guess, this is a bottom of a valley with slopes up to left and right. We soon felt our boots crunching on more clusters of spiky sweet chestnut cases. The floor becomes stony and then the path joins (at **5**, SR 9869 9713) a pine wood to the left with a stream on the right. You leave the woods through a gate with the National Trust plate and shortly arrive at the church of St Elidyr, or St James and St Elidyr (there are several churches named after Elidyr in south Pembrokeshire). This church has medieval origins but underwent

a major restoration in 1851 under the guidance of Sir George Gilbert Scott, the pre-eminent church architect of the time. He was the grandfather of Sir Giles Gilbert Scott, who designed Liverpool Cathedral and Battersea power station as well as the famous red GPO telephone box. The lychgate of the church displays the coat of arms with the inscription 'be mindful'. This is the motto of the Campbells of Cawdor, the former owners of the Stackpole Estate.

Continue the walk by returning into the woods, back down the path by which you arrived. Victorian artist and traveller Henry Thornhill Timmins walked this route at the end of the nineteenth century. It was a hot day and he was glad of the shade that the trees provided. He writes: *Pleasant it is, turning from the glare of the dusty roadway, to saunter beneath these leafy aisles of smooth-stemmed beech and knotty oak, mountain-ash, ilex and Scotch fir; and to push our way through intertwining thickets of bramble, wild-rose and ivy, enmeshed by the clinging woodbine and traveller's joy; while all the time the mercury, in less favoured spots, is climbing steadily towards the eighties.*

There was no sign of the thermometer reaching the eighties on the day of our visit, but at least the rain was keeping off. Pass the junction at **4**, walking along the bottom of the valley with pines to the left and mostly broadleaf trees to the right, until you emerge onto the road at **6** (9811 9650). Cross the road and look for the

gate on the far side and 20 yards or so to the right and go through the gate into Caroline Grove (Isabella Caroline Campbell was the wife of the first Baron Cawdor; they married in 1789). The trees here are mostly pines, at least to begin with. Pass the turning to your right (which will take you back to the car park) and take the board walk across the stream. You come to a stone arch on your right and a man-made cave with a log bench inside. The stones that make up this unusual structure are tunnelled with holes like Swiss cheese. One place we've seen stones like this is on weather-beaten rocky shores: pebbles sit in a small depression in a larger stone and wave action swirls the hard pebble around so that it  gradually drills a hole into the soft stone. The same kind of stones were used to construct a bench in the southern part of the Stackpole estate; perhaps these two features were made at the same time.

The pines have now given way to beech and holly; marshland with tall grasses appears on the left. Turn left at 7 (9771 9631) to cross the lake by a low causeway called the hidden bridge. To your right here across the water you can see the lovely 'one-arch bridge'. Turn right on the far side of the lake and then right again to follow the path along the shore, up towards the one-arch bridge. Here we met a couple walking several dogs with bells tied around their necks – 'so we know where they are', the couple told us. When you reach the bridge it is worth walking on to it to enjoy the view. If you carry on, the lane will lead you to the road with the car park, but a nicer route is to turn back off the bridge and head southwards along the tarmacked lane which bends to the right and takes you to an open space on the far side of which lies Stackpole Court.

Stackpole Court was the home to the Campbell's of Cawdor. This was one of the finest houses in Wales, home to a very wealthy family. There is little to see now - the house was demolished in 1963 and the good-looking clock tower is the most prominent thing remaining. The house was certainly still there at the time of Timmins' visit. He tells us that it had a massive porch flanked by two small Spanish cannons, named La Destruidora and La Tremenda. According to the book *Buildings of Wales*, the Lort family purchased the land here in 1611. Elizabeth Lort married Sir Alexander Campbell of Cawdor in Nairnshire in the Scottish

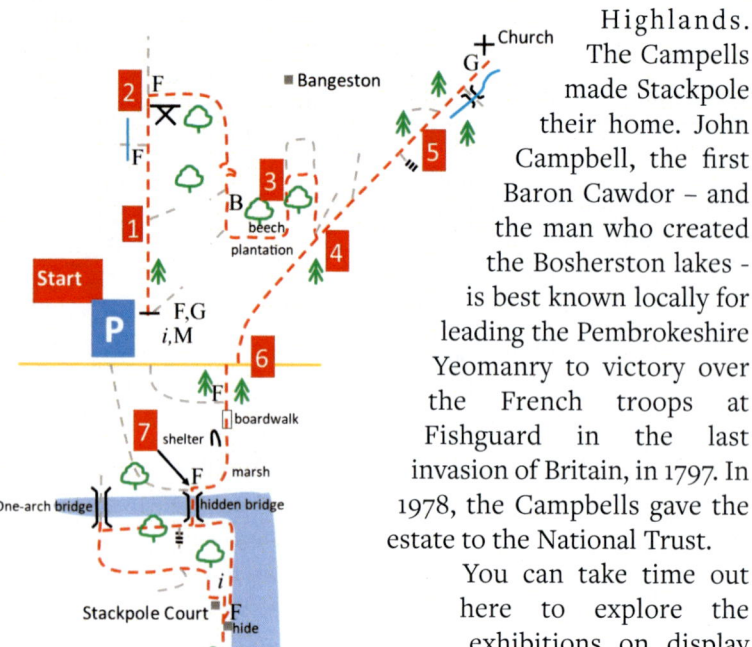

Highlands. The Campells made Stackpole their home. John Campbell, the first Baron Cawdor – and the man who created the Bosherston lakes - is best known locally for leading the Pembrokeshire Yeomanry to victory over the French troops at Fishguard in the last invasion of Britain, in 1797. In 1978, the Campbells gave the estate to the National Trust.

You can take time out here to explore the exhibitions on display and then, when you are ready, skirt round to the left of the clock building and follow signs to the lakes.

We walked up to the 8-arch bridge to touch the walk which comes next in this book (see Stackpole – southern section). We then retraced our footsteps, taking the path signposted 'one-arch bridge' by the bird hide and following the path back to the hidden bridge and on to the car park from there.

After the walk, the Stackpole Inn, in the small village of Stackpole, is worth a visit. It's more of a restaurant than a pub and it is popular so, if you want to eat, it is best to reserve a table. If you just fancy a drink, the beer is very well kept but the space to sit inside and drink is limited. Plenty of room outside, though. There is also the excellent walled garden café (see walk 17) if you just fancy a snack, a hot drink or a light meal.

Sweet Chestnut

They are not so common as they used to be, but braziers roasting chestnuts were once a familiar sight wherever crowds gathered on a winter evening in a large town or city. Roast chestnuts come from the sweet chestnut tree; horse chestnuts, the familiar conker, look similar but are inedible.

The leaves of the sweet chestnut tree are oval-shaped with serrated edges. The leaves can be long – up to 12 inches - and quite glossy. Each leaf is on its own stalk, unlike the horse chestnut whose leaves form in hand-shaped bunches. Sweet chestnut is not a native to these islands; it could have been introduced by the Romans, but no-one is quite sure. It is a mighty tree. According to the Woodland Trust, sweet chestnut trees can live for up to 700 years, the mature tree growing to 35 metres in height with a trunk two metres in diameter. Look out for the deep vertical fissures which spiral around the bark of a mature tree.

The nuts, in green spiky cases, fall to the ground in winter. They can be roasted in the oven to eat as they are and used in recipes including stuffing, nut roasts and cake fillings.

The Da Vinci Code

There are several accounts of Leonardo Da Vinci's idea (page 112) about the structure of trees, but none that we read tested his idea experimentally to see if it was right. In fact, the tone of some of the articles was that it would be too difficult to test: you would need to measure every branch in a tree to be sure. We weren't convinced about that. It seemed to us that you could get an idea about whether Leonardo was on the right track with a few simple measurements.

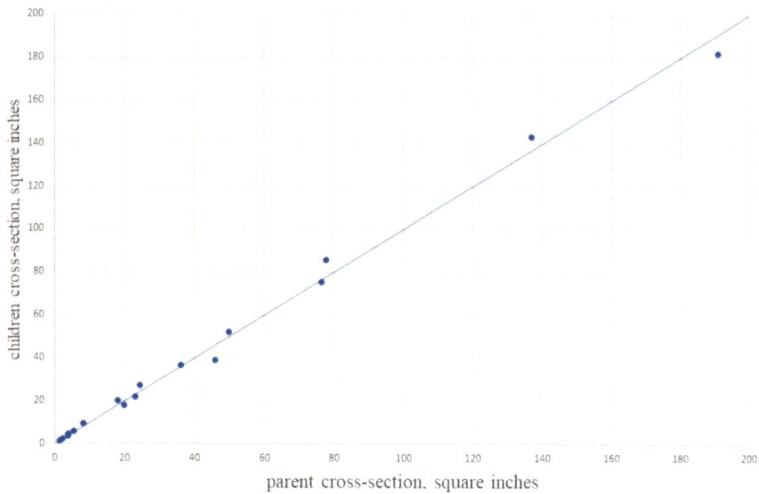

Da Vinci's idea, in essence, was that when a branch of a tree divides into two (or more) smaller branches, the total cross-sectional area of the 'children' would be the same as that of the parent branch. On our walks we took a piece of string and a tape measure and when we stopped for a rest we would get these out and take some measurements. We only measured branches which were close enough to the ground to reach and only living branches. It is possible that, subconsciously at least, we chose branches that *looked* as though they would fit the pattern. But, then, as our eye became practiced it *did* look as though most branches would fit the pattern.

We used the string to measure the circumference of the branch and calculated the cross-sectional area assuming that the branch was perfectly circular in section. The results are plotted out in the graph here. If Leonardo was right about the structure of trees, the points would lie on the 1:1 line, that is the cross-sectional area of the children would be the same as that of the parent. It's a good match and we are convinced that this makes a good model for tree structure. What a genius that man was.

| Walk 17 | **Stackpole** (southern section) |

A walk of 5 ½ kilometres, mostly on the flat, but with one gentle climb to a lookout point. Allow 2 hours.

Naturalist and TV presenter Iolo Williams' book *Wild Places* lists his choice of the top 40 nature sites in Wales. There is only one entry for mainland Pembrokeshire and it is Stackpole. Stackpole Woods are owned by the National Trust and are a National Nature Reserve managed by National Resources Wales. The freshwater lakes (the Bosherston Lakes, or lily ponds) for which the site is famous were created by dams in the 18th and 19th centuries.

According to Iolo, this is one of the best places in Wales to see otters close-up in the wild. There are also plenty of wading birds on display. This is a popular place - be prepared for dogwalkers galore and naturalists with telephoto lenses – but there is plenty of space and the site will soon swallow you up if you want to be on your own. The walk we have chosen takes you on a circuit around the shores of the lakes, mostly in woodland, and includes a visit to Broad Haven South, a lovely beach. The footpaths are well cared for, with plenty of signposts and information boards at regular

intervals. The terrain is mostly flat although walking boots are a good idea when the ground is muddy.

We parked at the Stackpole Centre (SR 976 957), the local administrative building for the National Trust. There is a parking charge for non-members of the NT, but this place is right at the heart of the nature reserve and the staff will tell you where to look for otters. You can also pick up a free map. Set off eastwards from the centre, through the car park and across the lane. Pass, on your left, the information board about this being a working estate and follow the zig-zag track down to the water's edge and the 8-arch bridge. This eye-catching bridge was built in 1797 by John Campbell, Lord Cawdor, who lived at Stackpole Court. The lakes themselves were developed by the Cawdor family in the late 18th and early 19th century.

It's worth getting your bearings here by walking onto the bridge to see what can be seen. What we saw, close up, was a grey heron,

standing very still apart from an occasional twist of its neck to look in a different direction. When you are ready to start walking, set off from the 8-arch bridge southwards under the trees along the west side of the lake. You are soon away from the world of roads and buildings, listening to the sound of songbirds in the trees and the croak of water birds. We passed an angler braving the rain. There was also, on this day, the distant sound of explosions from the nearby artillery range. Keep right at the grassy bridge **1** (SR 9757 9475) following the sign for Bosherston. The grassy bridge is actually a dam built around 1780 to create the first lake. South of the dam at that time was a tidal inlet which was subject to regular flooding. The problems caused by the flooding persuaded the estate owners to build a second dam at Broad Haven South and create extra lakes. The path becomes bare rock for a while here. Keep left at the 'central arm' signpost and cross the boardwalk with the wooden handrail at **2** (SR 9742 9470). Here are the famous lilies. Water lilies are a flowering plant, rooted in the soil beneath the lake, with leaves and flowers floating on the surface. The leaves are round, complete circles in some species and notched in others. The lilies flower between May and August and the best time to see them is in June and July.

The lakes are shallow and vulnerable to drought and low water levels during dry weather. The western lakes (the central and western 'arms' as they are called), beyond the grassy bridge, are filled mostly through springs in the lake floor. The water here is of good quality, filtered of silts and not over-rich in nutrients. The main 'eastern arm', though (the one with the 8-arch bridge) is fed by streams, bringing silt and nutrients from the land. In the confined area of the lake, the nutrients build up and give rise to unwanted algal blooms – mats of greenery which clog up the water and lower the levels of dissolved oxygen as they decay.

The low boardwalks are ideal for getting a good view of the water plants and birds and you will often hear a splash as fish jump. We watched a moorhen, with its red and gold-tipped beak, pecking away for food. Our guide to British Wildlife says that these birds are often wary, but this one seemed quite happy for us to be standing close and watching.

At the far side of the boardwalk, climb up the steps, ignoring the path to the left and you enter an area of open country with scrub and shrubs. Here you are crossing a raised promontory between the central and western arms of the lily ponds. After a little while on your right there is a noticeable clearing with an unmarked narrow path leading away across the grass. The path leads to the top of the promontory where there is an embankment typical of the iron age forts in Wales. The information board here hints that this may not have been, primarily, a military fortification. The tidal inlet that was here before the lakes would have made this an important trading point and the enclosure could have been used for storage, or keeping animals, or as a market place. A bronze pin, found in 1927, was probably brought here by traders.

Returning to the path, there is a viewpoint on the left which gives elevated views of the western arm. The path continues down steps from here. We passed a group of volunteers cutting back the hedges. They asked us if we'd seen the otters. Sadly not, we had to say. Continue to cross a second boardwalk with a wooden handrail at **3** (SR9686 9487). These boardwalks, standing on stone pillars, are a couple of feet above the water level most of the time but on occasions when the lake level is high, they can become submerged. One family told us about crossing this particular boardwalk in wellington boots, splashing through six inches of water, when a pike swam across the path in front of them, its long body spanning the width of the boardwalk.

On the far, southern, side of this lake crossing there is the option to take a detour to the village of Bosherston, where there is a café and a pub. Alternatively, continue along the path heading east on the south side of the lake. There are benches along this stretch if you need to rest for a while. Eventually, the path becomes sandy and brings you out onto the top of Broad Haven South beach.

There is a picnic bench at **4** (SR 9772 9436) and our eyes were drawn to a bright splash of colour on the end of the bench. Rain had rotted a small section of the wooden top and created a small depression which was home to a group of orange mushrooms (or toadstools). Amazing how nature can seize the smallest opportunity.

To get to the beach, cross the small wooden bridge (under which any excess water from the lakes flows to the sea) and create your own set of footsteps in the sand. Broad Haven South is a beach connoisseur's paradise. There are acres of pristine white sand backed by tall dunes. Along one side lie caves where you can change into your swimming costume or play hide and seek with

the children (best not at the same time). Swell waves arrive here from distant Atlantic storms and crash onto the beach. This has got to be one of the best beaches in Wales. And that's saying something for a nation which has some great beaches.

The view offshore is dominated by the stack, called (on OS maps) Church Rock, perhaps because of its steeple-like shape. The limestone cliffs here are gradually being eroded by the sea and Church Rock is a resistant remnant of where the cliffs used to be.

Leave the beach by the wooden bridge and follow the signpost to the eight-arch bridge. Ignore the turning towards Stackpole Quay on the right, but the next turning to the right is worth a short detour. There was a finger post here on our early visits, but it had been removed later on. In any case, the path is pretty clear. Follow this path to the top of the hill where there is an unusual dome-shaped seat, made of stones (at **5** SR 9773 9467). The year 1881 is carved into a flat stone above one of the seats – it is just possible to make it out. This must have been a place for Victorian ladies and gentleman to come and sit and look over the estate. You too can sit here and look over the woods.

We returned to the path towards the eight-arch bridge, walking initially through some low shrubs and ferns and then through trees with the lake on the left and sand dunes on the right. Cross the grassy bridge and turn right on the far side to retrace your steps back to the Stackpole Centre. And here, at last, were the otters. A chap walking a black Labrador pointed them out. 'They are on the edge of the reeds – one, two, no three of them'. They were too quick to get a photo, unfortunately (we need things to be big and slow for that, which is why this book is about trees) but we did catch what looked to us like a young heron watching us from the reeds.

After the walk, the café in the walled garden to the north-west of the Stackpole centre provides tea and snacks as well as cooked meals. You can eat indoors in poor weather or on outside tables when it is warm. There is also a marquee where you can sit with a pot of tea and a plate of cakes and talk about your experience. The charm of Stackpole is the opportunity of seeing wildlife close-up. It is like a zoo in which the inhabitants are free to come and go. Stackpole's wildlife is more animated than most animals in a zoo, probably because they are going about their business, hunting for food and avoiding being someone else's lunch. The experience of Stackpole is more than this, though. The soundscape is very special. Added to the usual sound of songbirds and the more raucous calling of the water birds, there is (on some days) the distant regular thunder of combers depositing their energy on the wonderful beach and the staccato chatter of machine-gun fire. It's hard to think of anywhere else, in Pembrokeshire and further afield, where you would get this combination of experiences. Fortunately, Stackpole's future seems secure and it will be there to enjoy it for years to come.

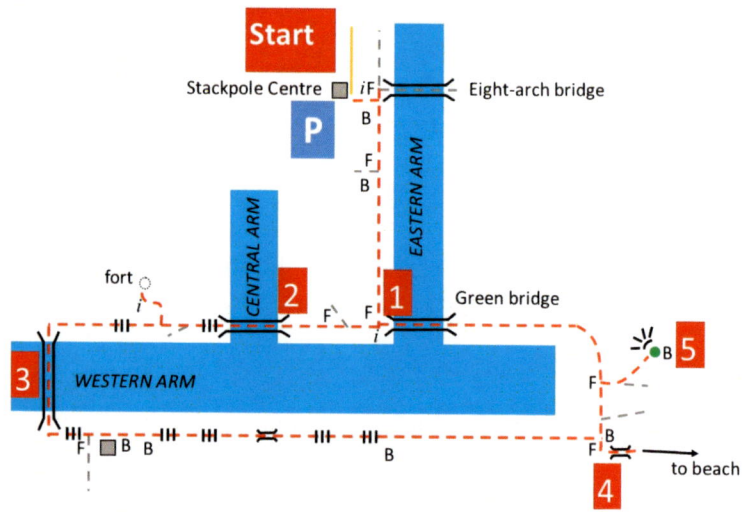

Green spaces

It has been estimated that there are around 3 billion trees in the United Kingdom.

This figure is based on measurements of forest area in aerial and satellite pictures and a guess at the space occupied by a single tree. We could probably add a few million more trees that live singly or in small groups in parks and gardens, as well as lining the avenues of city streets. There are, approximately, 50 trees for every person in the country. That sounds healthy. Most of us would be happy with 50 trees in our garden – and a garden big enough to stand them up. But, in fact, Britons are tree-poor. On a global scale, there is an average of about 500 trees per person. In European terms, the UK and the Irish Republic sit near the bottom of any table showing the proportion of land area that is covered in woodland.

The climate and topography of the British Isles are perfect for growing trees. Without human interference, mainland Britain would be mostly one big forest, stretching from the south coast of England up to the lowlands of Scotland with just the tops of the highest mountains and the most windswept coasts left bare. That is probably pretty much how things looked when the last land bridge between us and Europe disappeared under water about 8 thousand years ago.

Then the British started chopping down their trees. The timber provided fuel and building material and the cleared areas were used for growing crops and keeping livestock (and later for building towns, factories and cities). Very few trees were replanted and woodland cover steadily declined. By the beginning of the 20th century, just 5% of the land area of the UK remained as woodland.

The government now took decisive action to reverse this trend. In 1919, the Forestry Commission was established and new forests were planted. The forests appeared all over the country, particularly in Scotland, and included some very large ones. These new forests were different to the old ones: they were made up, mainly, of fast-growing evergreen trees: pines, spruce and fir (in general, conifers). Within 100 years, the proportion of tree coverage in the UK more than doubled to about 13% but nearly all of this increase was because of conifer trees. In Wales, for example, currently about half of all woodland trees are conifers.

Pembrokeshire has its share of these new forests. There are no particularly large ones, but they do reach a similar size to the largest deciduous forests in the county. The new forests may make money but they have never gained our affection. In several cases while researching this book, we came across signs that landowners were gradually replacing their conifers with native broadleaf species.

Woodlands have always had trouble with their bottom line. It is impossible to put a monetary value on the experience of walking in a traditional woodland, but there is plenty of value nevertheless. Where else can you walk under a soothing green canopy, hear birds singing above and beside you and feel the soft mulch of leaf mould beneath your feet? In spring there are broad swathes of bluebells and primroses. Woods provide sounds and sights that are pleasing to the human psyche. They appeal to us on some fundamental level, which has probably been developed over thousands of years of living on this planet with trees. We have been left with just a few scraps of the forest that used to cover these islands and if we are not careful, we will lose those. They would take a long time to replace. Woodlands are precious. They deserve our protection.

Bibliography

Connop-Price, M.R. Pembrokeshire: the forgotten coalfield. *Windmark Publishing, 2004.*

Fiennes, Peter. Oak and Ash and Thorn: The Ancient Woods and New Forests of Britain. *Oneworld Publications, 2017.*

Foot, David. Woods and People: putting forests on the map. *The History Press, 2010.*

Lloyd, Thomas, Orbach, Julian and Scourfield, Robert The Buildings of Wales: Pembrokeshire. *Cadw, 2004.*

Smith, Victor and Keith Smith. Western Main Lines. Carmarthen to Fishguard. *Middleton Press, 2020.*

Timmins, Henry Thornhill. Nooks and Crannies of Pembrokeshire. *Ellis Stock, 1895.*

Toulson, Shirley and Caroline Forbes. The Drovers Roads of Wales II: Pembrokeshire and the South. *Whittet Books Ltd., 1992.*

We were impressed with the Veritasium website which gives information about the science of trees, including the best explanation we could find of how water gets to the top of trees. https://www.youtube.com/watch?v=BickMFHAZR0

Acknowledgements

We are very grateful to all the organisations, public and private who protect and to maintain the woodlands of Pembrokeshire, to Myrddin ap Dafydd of Gwasg Carreg Gwalch for his support and to Lynwen Jones for putting this book together.